Infotech
English for computer users

Workbook

Santiago
Remacha Esteras

CAMBRIDGE
UNIVERSITY PRESS

CAMBRIDGE UNIVERSITY PRESS
Cambridge, New York, Melbourne, Madrid, Cape Town, Singapore, São Paulo

Cambridge University Press
The Edinburgh Building, Cambridge CB2 2RU, UK

www.cambridge.org
Information on this title: www.cambridge.org/9780521532884

First published 2003
4th printing 2006

Printed in the United Kingdom at the University Press, Cambridge

A catalogue record for this publication is available from the British Library

ISBN-13 978-0-521-53288-4 Workbook
ISBN-10 0-521-53288-4 Workbook

ISBN-13 978-0-521-75428-6 Student's Book
ISBN-10 0-521-75428-3 Student's Book

ISBN-13 978-0-521-75429-3 Teacher's Book
ISBN-10 0-521-75429-1 Teacher's Book

ISBN-13 978-0-521-75430-9 Audio Cassette
ISBN-10 0-521-75430-5 Audio Cassette

ISBN-13 978-0-521-75431-6 Audio CD
ISBN-10 0-521-75431-3 Audio CD

Contents

To the student

This Workbook gives you **extra practice** in the language you have learned in class. It is divided into 30 units, which relate to the units in the Student's Book.

You can use it to do particular exercises recommended by your teacher as **homework**; but you can also use it as a **self-study** book to revise grammar and vocabulary and to develop reading and writing skills.

There are four types of exercises:

Vocabulary

Vocabulary exercises give practice in the main areas of the unit. Sometimes the activity has the form of a **puzzle** or **word search**, which will help you remember the computer terms practised in the Student's Book. There are also **word-building** exercises which study word-formation processes (prefixes, suffixes, compounds); these will help you develop and extend your vocabulary in technical and general English.

- *If you don't know a technical term, you can look it up in the corresponding unit of the Student's Book or in the Glossary. You may also like to visit the Cambridge dictionaries website at* www.dictionary.cambridge.org *or an online computer dictionary on the Web, e.g.* www.webopedia.com.

Language work

Language exercises give practice in the main structures of English grammar. Sometimes they revise or complement the grammar points practised in the Student's Book. On other occasions, they focus on problem areas of grammar at intermediate level.

- *Read the Grammar boxes in the Student's Book and the Workbook before you do the exercises. It is a good idea to create your own Grammar record, in which you can make notes about important points, including examples.*

Reading

These sections contain reading tasks based on a variety of topics, from Internet history to new technologies such as robots, digital pens, flat screens, DVDs and MP3 music. The comprehension tasks will help you improve your reading skills.

- *You don't need to understand every word in a text. When you meet unknown words, try to guess the meaning from the context; it's also useful to work out what part of speech they are.*

Writing

These sections include different types of writing tasks: explaining diagrams, describing hardware, making advertisements, summarizing a text, writing e-mails and letters, making a web page, etc.

- *Try to write coherent texts, using appropriate linking words.*

At the back of the book you'll find a **list of irregular verbs** and the **answers** to the exercises.

The **cartoons** about computers and the Internet try to liven up the technical content of the book. I hope you enjoy them!

Don't forget!

The *Infotech* website at *www.cambridge.org/elt/ infotech* gives you more opportunities to develop your knowledge and language skills through the Internet.

- *You may like to have an Internet scrapbook where you can paste the best things from the Web.*

Unit 1 *Computer applications*

Language work: Present simple

1 **Read these sentences and match them with the uses of the present simple below.**

1 The conference starts at 10.
2 How often do you use computers at work?
3 She works as a media specialist.
4 Water freezes at 0 °C.
5 I usually read *Byte* magazine.
6 He likes coffee.
7 The sun rises in the east.

> Uses of the present simple:
> a permanent situations or states
> b permanent truths or laws of nature
> c a habit or something that happens regularly
> d a future, timetabled event

2 **Look at the table. Then ask and answer questions.**

e.g. *Does Gina read magazines? Yes, she does.*

	Read magazines	*Listen to MP3 music*	*Play computer games*	*Write e-mails*
Gina	✓	✓	✗	✗
Paul & Sue	✗	✗	✓	✓
You				

1 Gina   4 Paul and Sue   6 You
2 Gina   5 Paul and Sue   7 You
3 Paul and Sue

3 **Imagine you are interviewing your partner. Put these words in order to make questions.**

1 you/do/evenings/What/do/in the?
2 search/Do/the/information/you/on/Net/for?
3 films/type/of/What/like/you/do?
4 How/do/foreign/languages/you/speak/many?
5 you/strangers/chat/Do/on the Web/with?

Present simple

Affirmative
I/you/we/they   work
He/she/it   work**s**

Interrogative
Do   I/you/we/they
Does he/she/it   work?

Negative
I/you/we/they   don't
He/she/it   doesn't   work

In the third person singular we add **-s** to the base form. Exceptions: when the verb finishes in *-ss*, *-sh*, *-ch*, *-z* or *-o*, we add *-es*.

kiss	kisses	buzz	buzzes
wish	wishes	go	goes
watch	watches		

When the verb ends in consonant *+y*, we change the *-y* to *-ies*.

| study | studies | try | tries |

4 **Put these adverbs onto the lines below, according to the frequency.**

> rarely   always   often   usually
> sometimes   seldom   never

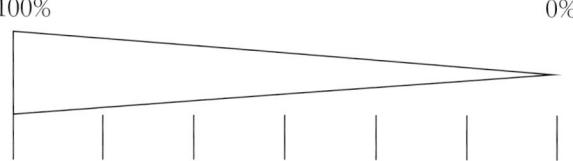

100%   0%

5 **Look at the next box. Rewrite these sentences with the adverbs.**

1 I receive SMS messages on my mobile phone. (*often*)
2 Jan sends articles to newsgroups. (*sometimes*)
3 Do you help your friends with their homework? (*usually*)
4 He is complaining. (*always*)
5 They have seen a UFO. (*never*)

Adverbs of frequency

They are usually placed:
- before the main verb, e.g. *Mary never goes to concerts.*
- after the verb *to be*, e.g. *She is always late.*
- if there is more than one auxiliary verb, they come after the first auxiliary, e.g. *This old computer has never been repaired.*

Other expressions used with the present simple
*I come to school **every Monday**.*
*I go to my office **on weekdays** / **on Tuesdays**.*
*She goes there **once** / **twice** / **three times a week**.*

Writing: How often?

6 **Write sentences about your friend, using one of these frequency expressions.**

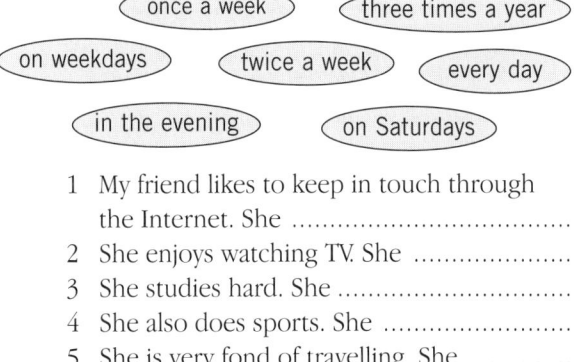

once a week   three times a year
on weekdays   twice a week   every day
in the evening   on Saturdays

1 My friend likes to keep in touch through the Internet. She ....
2 She enjoys watching TV. She ....
3 She studies hard. She ....
4 She also does sports. She ....
5 She is very fond of travelling. She ....
6 She likes going to the cinema. She ....
7 She loves pubs. She ....

Reading: Robots and androids

7 **Read the text and make a list of at least seven tasks done by robots and androids.**

"Hell of a day. The computer broke down and we all had to think."

8 **Refer to the text to find the term for these definitions.**

1 a science field that tries to improve computers and robots with features associated with human intelligence
2 programs used by computers
3 stage of mass production in which parts of a product move along for progressive assembly
4 small devices used for doing various tasks
5 robots that look like human beings

Robots and androids

Engineers are trying to make computers think and behave like humans. By combining Artificial Intelligence and engineering techniques, they're building different types of robots and androids.

Robots are devices that move and react to sensory input. They usually contain software that runs automatically without the intervention of a person. Today, they are used in all sorts of places, from factories to space exploration. We drive cars that have been welded by industrial robots. We buy products that have been made and packaged by robots in assembly lines. We use machines that have been built by robots.

Our life is affected by robotics in many other ways. Just think about medicine and the health system. Tiny computers are used to monitor the heart rate and blood pressure. Micro-machines and insect-sized robots help doctors in heart operations and other complicated surgery. Robots are used in dangerous situations – for example in repairing nuclear plants, cleaning toxic wastes, and defusing bombs.

Robotics has also been incorporated into the first 'intelligent homes'. There are gadgets that regulate the central heating, sensors that control the solar panels, robot maids that do the housework, etc.

Some research centres are building androids – robots that have the shape and capabilities of a human being. In the near future, androids will be available for sale. They will have access to the Internet, guide the blind and assist elderly people at home; they will be a 24 hour security guard for your home, sound the alarm in case of fire and phone the police if there is a burglary. In short, androids will become intelligent.

7

Word search: Parts of a PC

1 **Find 12 words about a computer system and its parts. They go down and across.**

D	R	I	V	E	B	R	A	M	F	H	P
L	S	O	I	R	A	H	M	E	I	A	L
O	R	S	C	A	N	N	E	R	D	R	M
W	L	P	X	Y	I	O	M	O	C	D	O
E	O	M	M	F	A	E	B	L	A	W	D
P	R	O	C	E	S	S	O	R	L	A	E
R	C	U	G	P	A	M	B	L	Z	R	M
I	D	S	D	R	R	O	M	I	R	E	Y
N	C	E	I	E	B	I	G	U	E	V	Z
T	R	I	S	E	M	O	N	I	T	O	R
E	R	S	K	X	Q	O	Z	X	Y	A	Z
R	R	E	T	S	O	F	T	W	A	R	E

Discourse: Classifying

2 **Look at the box. Then read the following paragraphs and underline the words and phrases that specify classification.**

There are three basic types of portable computers: (a) laptops, which run as fast as desktop PCs; (b) notebooks, which are as tiny as a notebook, and (c) handheld computers, which are used as Personal Digital Assistants. Some handheld PCs are hybrids, consisting of a phone and a PDA. Others include a small keyboard and a stylus to input data.

3 **Read these sentences and identify all classifying patterns. Then put them into the correct column.**

1 There are two classes of personal computers: (a) desktop PCs, and (b) portable PCs.
2 A computer system consists of two parts: hardware and software.
3 The basic structure of a PC is made up of three hardware sections: the CPU, the main memory and the peripherals.

4 The Control Unit, the ALU and the registers make up the CPU of a computer.
5 The RAM and ROM constitute the main memory.
6 A DVD is a type of disk.
7 A hub is a component of a computer network.

From general to specific	From specific to general
....	....
....	....
....	....
....	....

Classifying expressions

'Classifying' means putting things into groups or classes. For example, we classify sports, TV programmes, types of music, etc. This is also very common in computing.

We classify from the general to the more specific. For example, we say that '*computers (general) can be divided into five types: mainframes, mini-computers, desktop PCs, laptops and handheld computers (specific).*'

We can also classify from the specific to the more general. We say, for example, that '*a laptop (specific) is a type of computer (general).*'

Expressions used to classify from general to specific

... consists of   ... comprises
... is made up of   ... includes
... is composed of

... can be	classified		classes
... may be	divided	into	types
... are	categorized		groups

		types	
There are X	kinds	of ...	
	classes		
	categories		

▶

Expressions used to classify from specific to general

	a type of	
... is/are	an example of	
	a kind of	
	parts	
	components	

... constitute	... make up	... form

Writing: Explaining a diagram

4 **Study this diagram illustrating different types of peripherals. Write a description of the components and their uses.**

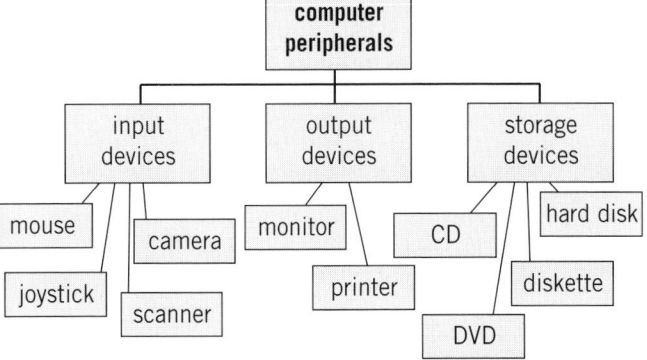

Useful constructions

- Active verbs describing the parts of a whole: *include, contain, constitute*
  e.g. *The peripherals **include** input/output devices as well as storage devices.*
- Passive constructions: *be composed of, be made up of, be divided into, be used to*
  e.g. *Storage devices **can be divided into two classes**: magnetic disks and optical disks.*
- Relative clauses
  e.g. *A webcam is a device **which is used** ...*

"I know we said we'd get you a laptop ... but this will have to do until business is better."

Reading: A digital pen

5 **Read this text and fill in the blanks with words in the box.**

sends	cables	computer	chip
digital	data	Internet	

Anoto is a (1) .... pen that allows you to store and transmit anything you write or draw on paper to any (2) ....

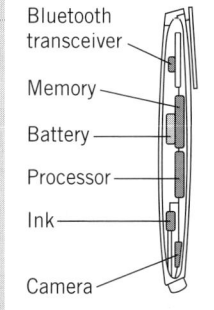

The components of *Anoto* are: (i) a digital camera, which scans the patterned paper, (ii) an image processor, (iii) a memory (3) ...., which can store several written pages, and (iv) a Bluetooth radio transceiver, which (4) .... the information to your PC, mobile phone or handheld computer. It also contains an ink cartridge so that you can actually see the characters and pictures that you are making.

Bluetooth transceiver
Memory
Battery
Processor
Ink
Camera

As you write or draw on the *Anoto* patterned paper, the digital pen converts your notes and diagrams into digital (5) .... which is stored and then transmitted to your computer or, by using a Bluetooth device such as a mobile phone, to another PC, database or the (6) .... Bluetooth is a wireless technology which doesn't need (7) .... in order to send and receive information.

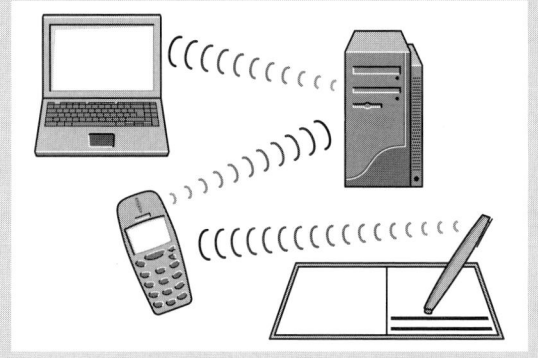

Vocabulary review: Abbreviations

1   **What's the meaning of these abbreviations?**

CPU   ....
ALU   ....
GHz   ....
RAM   ....
ROM   ....
DIMM ....

Language work: Relative clauses

2   **Read the text, and underline the relative pronouns and the words they refer to.**

The *Matrix* is a cyber-thriller which captures the audience's attention from the beginning. The movie, directed by the Wachowski brothers, has a storyline that combines action, science fiction, and special effects. The world is a virtual environment created by computers, where people are just slaves to AI machines which generate energy from human bodies.

Neo is a computer hacker that looks for an answer to the question 'What's the Matrix?' He discovers the truth when he meets the rebels Trinity and Morpheus. Trinity helps Neo and kills 'agents', who are really machines in human form. Morpheus shows Neo what the Matrix is – a reality beyond reality that controls human lives. The Matrix is protected by 'agents' led by Agent Smith, the character who tries to kill Neo.

Neo receives strong powers and becomes 'The One' who will liberate humankind from the evil artificial intelligence known as the Matrix. In the end, he kills Agent Smith and saves the humans. But ... does he really kill him? Find out in the next *Matrix* movie.

Trinity and Neo

3   **Read the examples of relative clauses again. Complete the rule with *that*, *who*, *which*.**

We use .... for people and .... for things.
We can use ..... for both people and things.

4   **Complete the sentences using *who*, *which*, *that*, *whose* or *where*.**

1   She works for a company .... main office is in Rome.
2   They've invented a digital video camera .... can be carried in the pocket of your jacket.
3   Do you know the school .... he studies?
4   The man .... married Sue is a millionaire.
5   She'll be responsible for anything .... goes wrong.

5   **Complete the definitions 1–6 using relative pronouns and the extra information in a–f.**

e.g. 1   *A barcode is a pattern of printed black lines **which** supermarkets use for prices.*

1   A barcode is a pattern of printed black lines
2   A CD-ROM drive is a common storage device
3   An anti-virus program is a type of software
4   A hacker is a person
5   A palmtop is a very small computer
6   A software engineer is a person

a   supermarkets use them for prices
b   he/she writes software
c   it reads data from a CD-ROM disk
d   it can be held in one hand
e   it protects your computer from viruses
f   he/she invades a network's privacy

6   **In which sentences can the relative pronoun be left out? Rewrite them without *who*, *that* or *which*.**

1   Have you got a video camera that I can use?
2   That is the girl who lives next door.
3   That is the girl who I met at the conference.
4   The police have arrested the hacker who broke into the computers of the Pentagon.
5   That's the film which I was talking about.
6   Have you read the report which Jack wrote last week?

7 **Read the box. Change these sentences to emphasize the words in *italics*.**

e.g. *Lucy* answered the phone.
It was Lucy who answered the phone (not Kim).

1 *Mary* broke your camera.
2 I saw a *spaceship*, not a UFO.
3 I bought a DVD *last Friday*.

Relative clauses

See the HELP box on page 13 of the Student's Book.

- We use **whose** to talk about possession.
  *This is my friend **whose** PC broke down last week.*
- We use **that** after indefinites (something, all, etc.)
  *Security is something **that** worries me.*
- When the relative pronoun is not the subject of the relative clause, we can omit it.
  The computer Ø we bought last week runs at 3 GHz.

Relative adverbs

The relative pronoun can be replaced by relative adverbs of **place** and **time**.
*This is the office **where** he works. (= ... at which)*
*I'll never forget the day **when** I visited Silicon Valley. (= ... on which)*

Emphasis with relatives

We can emphasize an element with **it is/was ... that ...**
Compare:
John sent Sally an e-mail last night.
***It was John that/who** sent Sally an e-mail last night. (not Paul)*
***It was Sally that** John sent an e-mail **to** last night. (not Mary)*
***It was an e-mail that** John sent Sally last night. (not a postcard)*
***It was last night that** John sent Sally an e-mail. (not this morning)*

Reading: Types of memory

8 **PCs use three types of memory: RAM, ROM and secondary storage. Read the text and decide which memory these features refer to.**

1 Any section of the main memory can be read with equal speed and ease.
2 It is available in hard disks, CDs, etc.
3 Part of this memory can be designated as 'cache'.
4 It stores basic operating instructions, needed by the CPU to function correctly.
5 It can be expanded by adding SIMMs.
6 Information cannot be deleted.
7 You can save your files.

Types of memory

The main memory of a computer is also called 'internal memory', as distinct from any storage memory available on disks. PCs make use of two types of main memory: RAM and ROM.

RAM stands for 'Random Access Memory'. It is called that because the processor can find data in any cell or memory address with equal speed, instead of looking for the data in a sequential order.

The data in the RAM is volatile, so it is lost when the power is switched off. Therefore, if we want to use this data later on, we have to save it on disk. When running an application, the CPU finds its location in the storage device (e.g. hard disk) and transfers a temporary copy of the application to the RAM area. Consequently, the size of RAM is vital when various programs are opened simultaneously or when a file is very complex.

The RAM capacity can be expanded by adding extra chips, which are contained in Single In-Line Memory Modules or SIMMs.

We can designate a certain amount of RAM space as cache in order to store data that a program uses repeatedly. A RAM cache may speed up our work, but we need a lot of memory or a special cache card.

ROM is an acronym for 'Read Only Memory', which implies that the processor can read and use the data stored in the ROM chip, but cannot put data into it. For this reason, it is also referred to as 'firmware'. ROM chips have 'constant' information, including instructions and routines for the basic operations of the CPU. These are used to start up the computer, to read the data from the keyboard or to send characters to the screen.

Unit 4 *Bits and bytes*

Vocabulary review: Units of memory

1 **Put these units of measurement in the correct place.**

terabyte   megabyte   gigabyte   bit
byte   kilobyte

Units of memory	Equivalence
1	binary digit (0 or 1)
2	8 bits
3	1024 bytes
4	1024 kilobytes
5	1024 megabytes
6	1024 gigabytes

2 **The quotations a–g below are typical in computing. Read them and find:**

1 the unit of measurement that represents ASCII characters
2 the abbreviation for 'megabyte'
3 the size of the text file
4 the acronym for 'random access memory'
5 the speed of a conventional modem
6 the maximum storage capacity of a DVD
7 the reason why you can't download an audio file

a
This text file occupies 3 kilobytes.

b A, z, 7
Bytes are used to represent individual characters – a letter, a number, or even a space.

c
I've got a Pentium computer with 512 megabytes of RAM and 80 gigabytes of hard disk space.

Word building: Prefixes

3 **Prefixes come before the root word and they usually change its meaning. Underline the prefixes in these examples and classify them according to the meaning.**

1 This TV programme is pre-recorded.
2 Some people consider number 13 unlucky.
3 My computer runs at 2 gigahertz.
4 The two firms are cooperating.
5 She travels to Barcelona on an intercity train.
6 Macroeconomics refers to the study of economics of a whole industry or country.

	Number:	....
	Time and order:	....
Prefixes	Location:	....
	Attitude:	....
	Size or degree:	....
	Negative:	....

4 **Look at the words in the box. Then match the prefixes 1–7 with their meaning a–g.**

> co-ordinate   anti-smoking   Internet
> subway   telephone   transmission
> reprint

1 co-   a over a distance
2 anti-   b against
3 inter-   c again, back
4 sub-   d across
5 tele-   e with, joint
6 trans-   f between, among
7 re-   g beneath

d
This Windows program runs best with 256 MB or more of memory.

f
You can't download this audio file. You need 3 MB of additional space on your disk.

e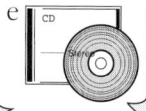
A CD can hold 650 megabytes of data. However, a DVD can store up to 17 gigabytes.

g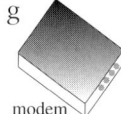
modem
A conventional modem transmits data at 56 kilobits per second.

5 Use the terms in brackets and the correct prefix (from exercise 4) to complete these sentences.

1 Press these keys to .... the computer. (BOOT)
2 I've bought an .... filter. It reduces the bright light and electromagnetic radiation. (GLARE)
3 DVD-Video technology supports eight languages and 32 .... (TITLES)
4 Some computer networks are .... via satellite. (CONNECTED)
5 A .... system displays information on a TV screen. (TEXT)
6 IBM, in .... with Apple and Motorola, created the PowerPC chip in 1993. (OPERATION)

6 Prefixes are commonly used in computer science. With the help of a dictionary, find two additional examples for each prefix.

Size or degree

super-	more than	super-computer	....
hyper-	extremely	hyper-media	....
mini-	small	mini-computer	....
micro-	very small	micro-computer	....
semi-	partly, half	semi-conductor	....
ultra-	beyond	ultra-modern	....

Number

uni-	one	unilateral	....
mono-	one	monochromatic	....
bi-	two	bidimensional	....
multi-	many	multi-user	....
kilo-	thousand	kilobit	....
mega-	one million	megabit	....
giga-	1,000 million	gigabit	....

7 Fill in the gaps with the correct negative prefix.

> unable illogical invisible misleading disagree

1 The chip is so small that it's almost
   ....
2 I .... with her proposals.
3 Unfortunately she is .... to help you.

4 The web advertisement gives a wrong idea about the product. It's very ....
5 This idea seems .... to me.

8 Add the correct negative prefix to these adjectives.

1 aware	4 rational	7 partial	9 honest
2 legitimate	5 perfect	8 practical	10 clean
3 patient	6 expected		

Negative prefixes

Negative	Meaning	Examples
un-	not	unfair, unbelievable
in-		incomplete, insane
im-		improbable, immoral
il-		illegible, illiterate
ir-		irrelevant, irresponsible
dis-		disloyal, dislike
non-		non-stop
un-	reverse action	undo, untie
de-	deprive of	debug, decompress
dis-		disconnect, discourage
mis-	wrongly	misinform, misinterpret
mal-	badly	malfunction, malformed

NOTES
- **un-** is usually found with adjectives that do not come from Latin (e.g. *unknown*)
- **in-** is common with adjectives originally from Latin (e.g *independent*)
- **in-** becomes **im-** when the adjective begins with **m** or **p** (e.g. *impossible*)
- **in-** becomes **il-** before *l* (e.g. *illegal*) and **ir-** before *r* (e.g. *irregular*)

"A virus ate my homework."

COMPUTER SCIENCE

Unit 5 *Buying a computer*

Vocabulary review: In a shop

1 **Look at these sentences and match them with the language functions a–g.**

1 Good morning. Can I help you?
2 Can I have a look at those pocket PCs?
3 It has a processor running at 3 GHz.
4 What about RAM?
5 Does it have a DVD?
6 Which one would you recommend?
7 How much does it cost?
8 Well, you can pay by cheque, credit card or in cash.

> a asking the price
> b describing a computer
> c asking to see some computers
> d greeting customers and offering help
> e asking about technical specifications
> f explaining different ways of paying
> g asking for advice

Reading: A portable computer

2 **Complete the text about a portable computer with the words in the box.**

> notebook microphone drive display
> CD peripherals anti-virus performance
> keyboard

3 **Read the text again and complete these notes with the most relevant information.**

> Microprocessor: ....
> RAM: ....
> Hard disk: ....
> Screen: ....
> Operating system: ....
> Other software: ....
> Other peripherals: ....
> Power supply: ....

The Toshiba Satellite only weighs eight pounds but it provides the power, (1) .... and multimedia functions of a desktop PC in a new mobile design. Packed with 3 GHz and 512 MB of RAM, the Satellite (2) .... is the perfect solution for those customers that want a multimedia portable computer at an affordable price.

Its 60 GB hard disk (3) .... is large enough to hold all the applications that you're likely to need. You also get a 3.5" internal floppy disk drive and a DVD/CD-RW unit compatible with most DVD and (4) .... formats.

It features a large 14.1" TFT active matrix (5) .... supporting up to 16 million colours at 1024 x 768 pixel resolution.

The Satellite comes with Windows XP pre-installed and additional software including Lotus SmartSuite, Adobe Acrobat Reader, Internet Explorer and an (6) .... program.

Its (7) .... has 85 full-sized keys with 12 function keys, and a touch pad pointing device acts as a mouse. The sound capabilities comprise a SoundBlaster card, built-in stereo speakers, and an external (8) .... port, so you can digitally record, edit and play back speech.

To get online, the Satellite has a 56k modem and an Ethernet connector. It can be connected to a wide range of (9) .... and network devices. It runs on rechargeable Lithium batteries.

Language work: Present progressive

4 **What are they doing?**

1 *He is inserting a CD-ROM into the disk drive.*

2 ....
....

3 ....

4 ....

5 ....

6 ....

5 **Present progressive for future plans.**
Look at the diary and correct the sentences
that are not true.

e.g. *He isn't meeting a client on Monday*
morning. He's visiting a car plant.

1 He's meeting a client on Monday morning.
2 He is showing some customers round the
   company on Tuesday.
3 He's having lunch with the production
   manager on Wednesday.
4 He's having a business meeting on Thursday.
5 He is inviting a wholesaler to play squash
   on Friday.
6 He's going to the theatre on Saturday.
7 His girlfriend is coming to see him on
   Sunday afternoon.

NOVEMBER	WEEK 46
Monday 11	visit car plant
Tuesday 12	fly to Los Angeles
Wednesday 13	lunch with sales manager
Thursday 14	do radio interview about the effect of technology on the environment
Friday 15	play squash with wholesaler
Saturday 16	go to the movies in the evening
Sunday 17	watch football match

Present progressive

We use the present progressive to talk about
- actions happening now
  Where is Carla? She's watching TV.
- temporary situations
  Greta is staying with her aunt for a few days.
- fixed arrangements in the near future (We often
  give the time, date or place.)
  I'm meeting Mrs Straw at 10.

6 **Choose the correct form – present simple**
or progressive.

1 A: What are you doing?
   B: I think / am thinking about his plan.
2 Do you have / are you having a webcam?
3 I don't know / am not knowing where she
   lives.
4 This perfume is smelling / smells of lemons.
5 Mary sees / is seeing her boyfriend; that's
   why she's wearing a new dress.
6 I hear / am hearing you are going on
   holiday soon.
7 Do you enjoy / are you enjoying this game?

Stative verbs

Stative verbs are not normally used in the
progressive form. They refer to permanent states
and not actions.
- Verbs of emotions: *love, like, enjoy, forgive,*
  hate
- Verbs of opinion: *think, understand, imagine,*
  agree
- Verbs of senses: *hear, see, smell, taste*
- Other verbs: *belong, contain, know, mean,*
  need, want

Some are used in the progressive form but there's
a difference in meaning. Compare As (states) with
Bs (actions):
1 *A He thinks it's important. (= he believes)*
  B She's thinking about it. (= she is considering)
2 *A He has a digital camera. (= he owns, possesses)*
  B She's having dinner. (= she is eating)
3 *A Do you see what I mean? (= do you*
  understand?)
  B I'm seeing Sue tomorrow. (= I'm meeting)
4 *A I enjoy MP3 music. (= I like in general)*
  B I'm enjoying this song. (= I like specifically)

Vocabulary review: I/O devices

1 **Look at the list of devices below.**
   a Translate the terms into your own language.
   b Which device would you use for these tasks?

1 to store data and programs
2 to type text into a computer
3 to read price labels in a shop
4 to click on hypertext links on Web pages
5 to show data on the screen
6 to enter drawings and sketches into a computer
7 to play computer games
8 to copy images from paper into a computer
9 to capture moving pictures and input them into a PC

Computer devices

a scanner	j keyboard
b monitor	k joystick
c ink-jet printer	l mouse
d hard disk	
e barcode reader	
f graphics tablet	
g DVD drive	
h digital video camera	
i microphone	

Reading: Electronic devices in shops

3 **Read through the text and find the answers to these questions.**

1 What's a barcode reader?
2 What types of information do barcodes represent?
3 What are the advantages of using barcode readers at a supermarket?
4 How does a computer system read the details on a credit card?
5 What type of card has a microprocessor inside, used for storing electronic money?

Describing function

We can describe computer devices in different ways.

A scanner
• A scanner is a **device that is used to** copy images from paper into a computer.
• A scanner is an input **device which copies** images from paper into a computer.

A joystick
• **You can use** a joystick **to** play computer games.
• A joystick is a device **for controlling and moving** the cursor around the screen in computer games.
• A joystick **is used to** play computer games. The user takes hold of a lever to move the cursor around the screen.

Language work: Describing function

2 **Describe the use of these devices in a paragraph. Use the structures from the box.**

    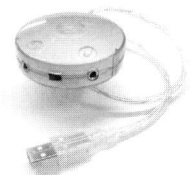

A printer..................... *A digital camera*.......... *A touch screen*............. *A microphone*..............

Electronic devices in shops

Different computerized systems make shopping easier for us. For example, supermarkets use **barcode readers/scanners** to read price labels. Customers use **smart cards** to pay for goods; and shops use **multimedia** systems to give information to their clients.

Barcode readers/scanners

A barcode reader is an input device that scans barcodes on the products sold in shops. Each package has a Universal Product Code or UPC, which consists of a series of dark bars and light spaces used to represent specific information about the product.

The **barcodes** are made of modules that represent binary digits, or bits. The first modules identify the general category of the product and the manufacturer. The next modules specify the product for the computer, including the brand name and the price. The last modules check that the information is read correctly.

ISBN 0-453-12148-9

9 780453 121484

When the **barcode scanner** reads the barcodes at the checkout counter, it sends the price to the computer in the cash register, where it is displayed on a screen and printed on a paper receipt. The data is also recorded on disk. Thus, computers can keep a record of what articles are in stock and can instantly give orders for new supplies.

Smart cards

We sometimes use **credit cards** to pay for goods. A computer system reads the details from a magnetic strip on our card and it checks the data with our bank account.

We also use **smart cards**. A smart card looks like a credit card but acts like a computer; the **microchip** embedded on the card stores monetary value, so we can use it to pay for products and services instead of cash. We can charge up the card at our bank, i.e. we can add digital cash and then use it to make phone calls or pay for newspapers, cinema and concert tickets.

4 **Match each term to the correct definition.**

1 barcode   a request to supply goods
2 cash register   b electronic money
3 order   c pattern of bars and spaces
4 smart card   d machine used for recording cash payments in shops
5 digital cash   e small plastic card which contains a chip inside

Writing: About barcode readers

5 **What are the potential benefits of using barcode scanners in these areas? Write down a paragraph for each one.**

EXAMPLE:

In boutiques, *barcode scanners can help the shop assistant to read the price labels of articles (clothes, cosmetics, hats, etc.). The data is also sent to the computer's inventory records.*

In bookshops, …

In pharmacies, …

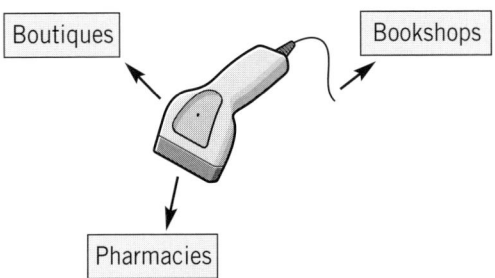

Boutiques

Bookshops

Pharmacies

Language work: Comparison

1 **Fill in the blanks with the correct comparative and superlative forms.**

e.g. *hard*   *harder*   *the hardest*

1 long ....
2 boring ....
3 wet ....
4 good ....
5 attractive ....
6 pretty ....
7 modern ....
8 exciting ....

2 **Use the adjectives and write comparisons as in the example.**

e.g. *comfortable expensive fast big*

A car is more comfortable than a motorbike.
A motorbike is less expensive than a car.
A car is faster than a motorbike.
A motorbike isn't as big as a car.

1 big   powerful   heavy   fast

A desktop PC is ....
A laptop is ....
A desktop PC is ....
A laptop is ....

2 intelligent   patient   sensible   strong

Women ....
Men ....
Women ....
Men ....

Making comparisons

a You form the comparative of **one-syllable** adjectives with **-er** and the superlative with **-est**.
slow   slower   the slowest
high   higher   the highest
*Ink-jet printers are **slower than** laser printers.*
*Imagesetters produce **the highest** resolution.*
• Adjectives with one vowel followed by one consonant double the consonant.
big   bigger   the biggest
• **Than** is used after comparatives. Don't use **that**.
• After superlatives, we do not use **of** with a singular word for a place or group.
*This is the fastest chip **in the world**.*
NOT ... ~~of the world~~
BUT ... *the fastest chip of all.*

b Adjectives with **three or more syllables** form the comparative with **more/less** and the superlative with **most/least**.
accurate   more accurate   the most accurate
Flatbed scanners are more accurate than handheld scanners.

c **Two-syllable** adjectives usually take **more/less**.
more modern   more advanced
• But those adjectives ending in **-y** (e.g. *happy, easy*) take **-er** and **-est**, and the 'y' changes to 'i'.
*Impact printers are **noisier** than non-impact printers.*

d Note the **irregular** forms:
good   better   the best
bad   worse   the worst
little   less   the least

e You can make comparisons in **different ways**.
CD-ROMs are cheaper than DVDs.
or *DVDs are **more** expensive **than** CD-ROMs.*
or *CD-ROMs are **not as/so** expensive **as** DVDs.*
or *CD-ROMs are **less** expensive **than** DVDs.*

We use **as ... as** to compare things that are equal.
My digital camera is as good as yours.

3 Complete these sentences using the superlative of the adjectives in brackets.

1 Dracula is the (popular) .... character in horror films.
2 The Pacific is the (large) .... ocean.
3 American people elect the (influential) .... President in the world.
4 The (small) .... keyboard was invented by David Levy in 1997.
5 The HP Pocket PC is the (powerful) .... Personal Digital Assistant.
6 The 'I love you' computer bug is the (bad) .... virus in history.

4 Decide who or what you would nominate for

1 the most interesting person you've ever met
    ....
2 the most exciting film you've ever seen
    ....
3 the best football team
    ....
4 the funniest TV programme
    ....
5 the most intelligent student in your class
    ....
6 the most dangerous sport
    ....
7 the most popular Internet program
    ....
8 the least difficult foreign language
    ....

Comparison with adverbs

The comparative and superlative of **adverbs** follow similar rules. For example:
*My computer operates **faster than** yours.*
*I can type **more easily** on this keyboard **than** on the other one.*
*I work **best** on a large screen.*

Special cases of comparison

You can also use **too** + adjective, or **not** + adjective + **enough** to make comparisons:
*This problem is **too difficult** for me. = This problem is **not easy enough**.*

---

5 Write the comparative or superlative of an adverb from the box for each blank.

fluently	hard	late	beautifully
early	badly	fast	neatly

1 Lisa speaks German the .... of all the girls in my class.
2 Twelve is very late, could you get here ....?
3 Jane works .... than Beth.
4 My uncle cooks .... than my aunt.
5 He arrived .... than usual, so he missed the train.
6 Fred can run the .... in his class.
7 Which girl sings ...., do you think?
8 I write .... than my sister.

6 Look at these sentences.

The room was too small. = The room was not big enough.

Decide which rules are correct.

1 *too* comes before an adjective or adverb.
2 *enough* comes before an adjective or adverb.
3 *enough* comes after an adjective or adverb.
4 *too* comes after an adjective or adverb.

7 Rewrite these sentences using the words given.

1 She is too young to do everything she wants. (not enough) ....
2 My Internet connection is not fast enough. (too) ....
3 The laser printer wasn't cheap enough. (expensive) ....

Writing: Comparing countries

8 Write six differences between the USA, China and your country.

How not to look after your PC

Vocabulary review: The monitor

1 **Solve the clues by using a term from the list.
Then complete the puzzle to find the hidden phrase.**

| pixels | card | flicker | beam | filter | refresh |
| resolution | display | hertz | contrast |

1 Screens with a low .... rate can produce eye fatigue.
2 Pictures which use a lot of pixels are high ....
3 Inside the tube there is an electron .... which scans the screen and turns on or off the pixels.
4 Some monitors have an anti-glare .... to reduce glare.
5 A monitor is also called a visual .... unit.
6 The .... on a CRT monitor is tiring on the eyes.
7 A video .... allows graphics to be displayed on your computer.
8 Characters and pictures are made up of dots, also called ....
9 This monitor has a 75 .... refresh rate.
10 Brightness and .... buttons let you alter the image.

Reading: Flat screens

2 **Read the text and then decide whether these statements are true or false.**

1 Most computers still use CRT monitors.
2 Typical CRT-based displays occupy less space than LCD displays.
3 Liquid-crystal displays are curved.
4 Flat LCD screens are becoming very popular.
5 LCD technology consumes less power than CRT technology.
6 Flat screens are cheaper than CRT monitors.
7 Users of flat-screen monitors can't adjust the angle of vision.

Flat screens

Have you noticed how much your computer screen flickers? This may be because your computer monitor uses CRT technology. This kind of technology offers colour and high-resolution pictures for relatively little money but the monitors are large, use a lot of energy, can flicker and emit electromagnetic radiation.

In recent years flat screens have become increasingly popular. Users talk of benefits such as more desk space, how easy they are to adjust for tilt and height, clearer images and the total elimination of screen flicker. It's like having a different PC, a new window on the world.

Most flat screens are based on LCD technology which has a lot of benefits over CRT technology. Among them:
• LCDs are inherently flat, CRT monitors are not, so LCDs require much less space.
• LCDs use less power than CRTs.
• LCDs are distortion-free while typical CRTs are curved, which may cause image distortion.
• most LCD displays use a TFT system offering a wider angle of vision and high-quality images.

But there is one major drawback to flat screens: their cost. They are expensive compared with CRT monitors. Prices are falling, however, and they'll soon find their way into homes, schools and businesses.

Flat screens usually include built-in stereo speakers, headphone connection, and a USB port. Some models can also be removed from the stand and mounted on the wall. They come with stylish designs for a variety of applications. LCDs range from small-size PC screens and TVs to large-screen projectors.

3 **Find these abbreviations in the text. Do you know what they stand for?**

CRT ....

LCD ....

TV ....

PC ....

TFT ....

USB ....

Language work: Modal verbs 1

4 **Imagine that you're helping a friend to buy and use a computer. Add two more DOs and DON'Ts to the list. Then rewrite the sentences with *should* or *ought to*.**

DO

1 a *If you need space on your desk, choose an LCD flat screen.*

   b *You should / ought to buy an LCD flat screen if you need space on your desk.*

2 a ....

   b ....

3 a ....

   b ....

DON'T

1 a *Don't buy a PC that hasn't got an optical drive.*

   b *You shouldn't / oughtn't to buy a PC that hasn't got an optical drive.*

2 a ....

   b ....

3 a ....

   b ....

5 **Complete these sentences. Use *should / had better* or *shouldn't / had better not*.**

1 You .... open the monitor. It's dangerous.

2 You drive much too fast. You .... be more careful.

3 You .... smoke so much. It's bad for your health.

4 You .... leave enough space behind the monitor for unobstructed movement.

5 You .... check your hard disk for viruses.

6 **Which sentences have a similar meaning?**

1 You have to be back home at 10.

2 You don't have to be back home at 10.

3 You must be back home at 10.

4 You needn't be back home at 10.

7 **Complete these sentences. Use *have to*, *needn't* or *mustn't*.**

1 We .... buy any disks. We've got enough.

2 You .... use a monitor that is fuzzy or distorts the image.

3 In the UK, many students .... wear a uniform at school.

4 Sarah .... send this fax. The boss told her to.

5 You .... touch that switch; it's dangerous.

6 You .... pay for this, it's free.

Modal verbs 1

Instructions and advice

- We use the imperative to give instructions.
  Keep the disks away from the sun.
- We use **should** or **ought** to give advice.
  You shouldn't stare at the screen for long periods of time. (= You ought not to stare ...)
- Another way of giving advice is **had better** + infinitive without **to**.
  You had better tell her that you've borrowed her CDs, or she'll be furious.

Necessity and obligation

- We use **need to**, **have to** and **must** to describe obligation and necessity.
  *We **need** to be at the airport by 8.30.*
  *You **must** remember to lock the office door.*
- We use **don't need to**, **don't have to** or **needn't** (without **to**) to say that something is not necessary or obligatory.
  *You **needn't** worry about the test. (= **You don't need to / don't have to** worry ...)*
- We use **mustn't** to express prohibition.
  *This is secret. You **mustn't** tell anyone.*

REMEMBER!

- Don't use **mustn't** to express absence of obligation.
- Don't use **don't have to** to express prohibition.

21

Reading: Printer languages

1 These statements are all false. Read the text and correct them.

1 HP printers do not understand the PCL language.
2 PostScript was created in the late 1980s.
3 Scalable fonts cannot be enlarged or reduced.
4 The 'script' of a PostScript file contains the sub-routines used to form different graphic elements.
5 PostScript is not understood by imagesetters.
6 PostScript doesn't support audio and video formats.

2 Match the terms (1–5) with the correct definitions (a–e).

1 printer language   4 imagesetter
2 scalable font   5 Raster Image Processor
3 emulate

a device which converts PostScript into images or text that can be printed by an imagesetter
b language that describes how to print the text and images on each page
c to make one printer act in the same way as another
d system that can produce characters of any size
e type of printer that generates output at very high resolution, on paper or film

Printer languages

Computers use a page description language or PDL to describe the layout and contents of a printed page. The best-known PDLs are Adobe PostScript and Hewlett Packard PCL (Printer Control Language), both of which
5 are used to control laser printers. For dot-matrix printers, a common language is the Epson command set.

Both PostScript and modern versions of PCL are object-oriented, meaning that they describe a page in terms of geometrical objects such as lines, arcs, and circles.

10 **PCL (Printer Control Language)**

This language was developed by Hewlett Packard and is used in many of their laser and ink-jet printers (e.g. *LaserJets* and *DeskJets*). The latest versions support a scalable font technology called Intellifont.

15 The representation of the font defines the shape (or outline) of each character. The scalable font can then enlarge or reduce the character to any size, without distortions.

Other manufacturers design
20 their printers so that they understand PCL, making them able to emulate HP printers. In this way, their printers are HP-compatible.

PostScript

PostScript was created by Adobe Systems Inc. in 1982 as 25
a PDL for laser printers and imagesetters. Like PCL, PostScript works in vectorial format, which means that it stores graphics not as images made up of dots but as geometric descriptions. This allows text and graphics to 30
be modified with no loss of quality.

A PostScript file consists of two main parts: the 'prolog', which contains a set of sub-routines used to form different graphic elements (squares, curves, etc.), and the 'script' which contains the elements introduced by 35
the user. The script calls up the sub-routines stored in the prolog and adds the parameters: for example, if you have drawn a square of 10 x 5 cm, the script calls up the sub-routine square and specifies the values 10 x 5.

PostScript is device-independent, which means that it can 40
speak to different output devices (printers, imagesetters, film recorders) and adjust the quality to the highest capability of the devices. In imagesetters, the hardware that interprets the code is called Raster Image Processor.

Drawing programs such as *Illustrator*, *Freehand*, or 45
CorelDraw produce pictures drawn in PostScript directly. PostScript has support for sound, video and other formats: you can mix scanned images, specify half-tone screens and introduce any number of effects. In fact, the only barrier is your imagination. 50

Discourse: Cohesion techniques

3 **Look at the box. Then read the text again and note down examples of these lexical cohesion techniques.**

1 Repetitions: ....
....

2 Synonyms: ....
....

3 Collocations: ....
....

4 Superordinates and hyponyms: ....
....

4 **Look back at the text to find out what the underlined words refer to.**

1 ..., both of which are used to control laser printers. (lines 4–5)
2 ... used in many of their laser and ink-jet printers (line 12)
3 ... it stores graphics not as ... (lines 28–9)
4 This allows text and graphics to be modified ... (lines 30–1)
5 ... and the 'script' which contains the elements introduced by the user. (lines 34–6)
6 ..., the hardware that interprets the code is called Raster Image Processor. (lines 43–44)
7 Drawing programs such as *Illustrator*, *Freehand*, or *CorelDraw* ... (lines 45–6)

Cohesion techniques

Lexical cohesion
The words chosen by a writer or speaker give internal cohesion to texts. There are various techniques.

- Repetitions
  *Once upon a time there was a king. The **king** had two sons ...*
- Synonyms (words with a similar meaning)
  *This worksheet shows the **income** and expenses of the company. The total **revenue** is ...*
- Collocations
  These are words which frequently go together, e.g. *RAM memory   floppy disk   browse the Web*
- Superordinates and hyponyms
  Superordinates are general words, e.g. *printer*
  Hyponyms are subdivisions of the general category, e.g. *dot-matrix, ink-jet, laser printers*

Reference signals
These point to something else in the text.
- Referring back:
  – personal and possessive pronouns: *he, his, ...*
  – determiners: *the, this, previous, above, ...*
  | Bill Gates | *knew that* | PCs | *would be big business and he imagined Microsoft playing a central role in this industry. His aim ...*
- Referring forward: *this, these, following, below, ...*
  Perhaps I shouldn't tell you this, but I don't know how a scanner works.
  The results can be seen in the table below.

Writing: An advertisement

5 **Choose one product from the list below and follow the guided steps to write an advertisement.**

Products:
- a digital camera
- a colour ink-jet printer
- a webcam

Write down your notes in these steps.

1 The **product** we are going to advertise is
....
It is used: ....
It is aimed at: ....
Its advantages over rival products are:
....
2 We have chosen the following **name**:
....
3 The most suitable medium for advertising is:
- The Internet
- Television/Radio
- National or local paper
- Specialist magazine for computer users
Reasons for this choice: ....
Images or atmosphere that could be associated with the product: ....
4 The **slogan** for the product is: ....

Now use your notes and some persuasive vocabulary to write a complete advertisement. Don't forget to use cohesive devices.

▶

Vocabulary review: Assistive technology

1 **Complete the sentences with suitable compounds from this list.**

expansion slots	database	websites
word processor	magnification software	
voice recognition	screen reader	

1 .... can enlarge text appearing on the screen by up to 16 times.
2 Blind users can't use a typical .... to write letters or faxes. They need Braille and a speech-synthesis system.
3 A .... allows blind users to hear the text from the screen.
4 .... interprets human speech, transforming the words into digitized text.
5 .... let users install expansion boards (modems, graphics boards, etc.) to improve the computer system.
6 A .... contains a set of structured data.
7 There are .... which give information about assistive technologies for the disabled.

Word building: Compound nouns

2 **Think of suitable compound nouns for these definitions.**

EXAMPLE: *A device which displays or prints the output*
ANSWER: *An output device*

1 A secret word used to receive e-mail
....
2 A pool that we swim in
....
3 A book which has cheques
....
4 A room where you eat meals
....

5 Lights used to control the traffic
....
6 A card used instead of coins to make phone calls ....

Compound nouns

Compound nouns consist of two or more bases. They are very common in technical English, e.g. *computer virus.*

In a compound noun there is a **headword** and one or more words that act as **modifiers**.

computer software	industry
modifiers	headword

Modifiers can refer to different things:
– the **material**
  gold medal = medal made of gold
– the **use or function**
  storage device = a device used for storage
– the **activity**
  software developer = a person who develops software

1 noun + noun

access time	*joystick*
lightpen	*address book*
mail merge	*computer mouse*
credit card	*palmtop*

2 verb or verbal noun + noun

flashlight	*flowchart*
scan rate	*typing paper*
mailing list	*recording head*

3 adjective + noun

hardware	*floppy disk*

- A defining noun in a compound is normally **singular**.
  a record shop = a shop that sells records
  However, we say *clothes shop* and *sports shop*.
- Some compound nouns are written as **one word**. Others are written as **two words** or are **hyphenated**. Unfortunately there are no rules. For example, we can find 'website', 'web site' and 'web-site'.

bookmark	*barcode*
bulletin board	*ink-jet printer*
firewall	*domain name*

▶

Pronunciation

Compounds normally contain a primary accent on the first element and a secondary accent on the second.

ˈaccess ˌtime   ˈlaser ˌprinter
/ˈækses ˌtaɪm/   /ˈleɪzə ˌprɪntə/

There are exceptions, so it's a good idea to check in a dictionary.

3   Explain the following compounds as in the examples.

silicon chip = a chip which is made of silicon
webmaster = a person who maintains a website

1   software programmer

....

2   disk drive

....

3   file server

....

4   systems analyst

....

5   input device

....

6   laser printer

....

7   bookshop

....

4   Making wordwebs will help you to organize and remember vocabulary. Use the words in the box to make three different wordwebs with compounds.

| floppy   error   mail   share   word |
| optical   free   firm   pal   site   drive |
| soft   designer   hard   directory |
| page   compact |

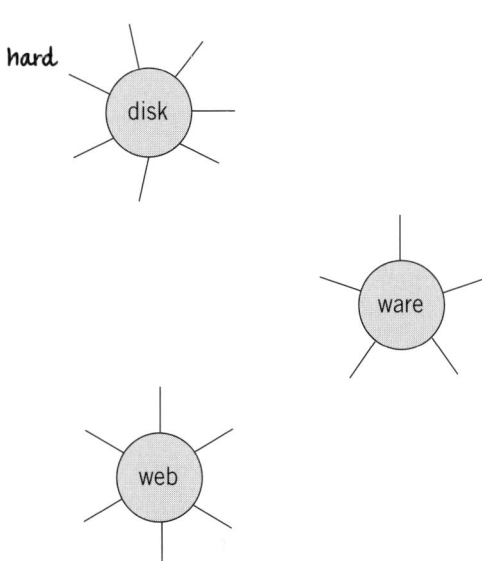

Unit 11 *Magnetic drives*

Vocabulary review: Disks

1 Choose a word from the network to complete the sentences.

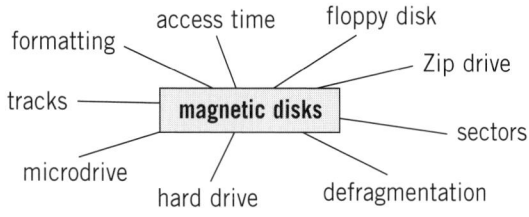

formatting — access time — floppy disk
tracks — **magnetic disks** — Zip drive
microdrive — hard drive — sectors — defragmentation

1   A high-density .... can hold 1.44 MB.
2   PCs usually have one .... called C.
3   A .... is a type of removable drive.
4   The smallest hard drive is known as a
     .... ; it's used for digital cameras.
5   .... means preparing a disk to
     receive data.
6   Once a disk is formatted the data can be
     recorded in disk .... and
     ....
7   The average time required for the
     read/write heads to move and access data is
     called ....
8   A .... program will help you
     reorganize the broken up files into
     contiguous sectors of the hard disk.

Word building: Suffixes

2 Read the sentences below. Underline the suffixes. Then decide what part of speech each word is: *noun, verb, adjective* or *adverb*.

>   adj   adj   noun   adverb
> e.g. *Person**al** Digit**al** Assist**ants** are increasing**ly** popular.*

1   A service provider usually charges a
     monthly fee for Internet connection.
2   Erasable optical drives are more expensive
     than magnetic drives.
3   If you like electronic entertainment, you
     can play online with other users.
4   We use the Web to search for information,
     visit virtual museums, do the shopping, etc.

3 Put the words in the box into the correct column.

threaten	measurement	quickly
electronically	partnership	criticize
disinfectant	eastward	colourful
clockwise	harmless	stimulate
journalist	affirmative	dirty	purify

Nouns	*Verbs*	*Adjectives*	*Adverbs*
....	....	....	....
....	....	....	....
....	....	....	....
....	....	....	....
....	....	....	....

Suffixes

Suffixes change the word class of the root word: for example, by adding the suffix *-ation*, the verb *compile* is changed into the noun *compilation*.

	Meaning	Examples
Noun suffixes		
-er/-or	agent	teacher/actor
-eer	occupation	engineer
-ess	female	waitress
-hood	status	brotherhood
-ance	quality of	assistance
-ence	quality of	independence
-ist	occupation	typist
-ian	occupation	electrician
-ing	activity	multi-tasking
-ment	state, action	amazement
-ness	state, quality	happiness
-ity	state, quality	security
-ion	state, action	compression
-tion, -ation	state, action	institution
-ism	attitude, state	magnetism
-ant	agent	assistant
-dom	state	freedom
-ship	state	relationship
Verb suffixes		
-ize (-ise)	to make	magnetize
-ify		simplify
-en		widen
-ate		activate

▶

Adverb suffixes

-ly	in a ... manner	logically
-ward(s)	direction	backward(s)
-wise	in the manner of	crabwise

Adjective suffixes

-ful	having ...	careful
-less	without ...	careless
-ly	having the quality	friendly
-al	of ...	musical
-ive		sensitive
-ic		scientific
-ical		electrical
-ing		exciting
-able		comparable
-ible	of being ...	reducible
-ish	like ...	foolish
-ous	full of ...	mysterious
-y	covered with ...	creamy

4 **Form the <u>noun</u> from each verb using one of these suffixes: *-ment, -ing, -ance, -ation.***

1 advertise ....
2 program ....
3 employ ....
4 meet ....
5 perform ....
6 resist ....
7 organize ....
8 attach ....
9 process ....
10 compile ....
11 transform ....
12 develop ....
13 imagine ....
14 insure ....

5 **Form the <u>adjective</u> using one of these suffixes: *-al, -ful, -ous, -able, -ive.***

1 danger ....
2 help ....
3 power ....
4 profession ....
5 success ....
6 person ....
7 attract ....
8 negotiate ....
9 create ....
10 interact ....
11 enjoy ....
12 protect ....

6 **Look at the groups of words and decide what part of speech each word is. Then complete the sentences with the correct word.**

| compute | computer | computerize |
| computation | computational | |

1 We need more money to .... the school library.
2 A bug in the program caused a .... error.

3 CAD means .... -aided design.

| browse | browsing | browser |

4 The most widely used .... is Internet Explorer.
5 .... means surfing or exploring the Web.
6 Most of the time, we .... the Web by clicking on hyperlinks.

Writing: Completing an advert

7 **Complete this advert for the MegaMind hard disk with the words in the box.**

gigabytes	drive	compatible
highest	time	protection	secure
visit	multimedia		

MegaMind XT

Today's personal computers are very powerful, but to handle large applications like databases, (1) .... , DTP publishing and CAD, you need to put more than 4 (2) .... in your hard disk. That's where MegaMind XT comes in. A reliable hard (3) .... with 80 gigabytes of capacity; average seek (4) .... of 8 milliseconds and a data transfer rate of 13 megabits per second; with a 3.5" drive unit and a five-year warranty.

You also receive software utilities that let you easily manage and (5) .... your data. Our software provides formatting, partitions, disk optimization and password (6) ....

MegaMind XT is (7) .... with IBM PCs as well as Macintosh computers. As with every MegaMind product – hard disk or optical – the XT delivers you the (8) .... performance. So call up today on 0208 796 0402. Or (9) .... our website at www.megamind.com.

Unit 12 *Optical breakthrough*

Reading: DVD technology

1 **Read the text and match these headings to the correct paragraphs.**

DVD formats   DVDs versus CDs   What's a DVD?
Configurations of data layers   Looking forward

1 ....

DVD stands for **d**igital **v**ersatile **d**isk. It's essentially a new type of compact disk which can hold several gigabytes of multimedia elements – video, audio and computer data. DVD uses MPEG-2 to compress video.

2 ....

At first sight a DVD is similar to a CD. Both disks are 120 mm in diameter and 1.2 mm thick. They *also* use a laser beam to read data. *However*, they are very different in internal structure and data capacity. In a DVD the tracks are very close in space, *thus* allowing more tracks per disk. The distance between each track is 0.74 micron, *whereas* in a CD the track pitch is 1.6 micron. *In addition*, the pits in which data is stored are smaller, *so* there are more pits per track. *Furthermore*, DVDs can be double-sided, which doubles their potential storage capacity.

3 ....

A **DVD-ROM** holds computer data and is read by a DVD-ROM drive in a computer. DVD-ROM drives are backward-compatible, so they can also play old CD-ROMS, video CDs and CD-R disks.

A **DVD-Video** disk is the best storage medium for full-length movies. It can support eight different languages, 32 subtitles, and various audio formats. DVD-Video players are connected to TV sets.

A **DVD-Audio** disk contains sound files, supporting PCM digital audio, Dolby Digital and DTS, a high-quality audio format used in theatres.

Recordable DVDs come in various formats: DVD-R disks are similar in concept to CD-R (Recordable), i.e. they can record data only once, while the rewritable formats (e.g. DVD-RAM and DVD+RW) can be erased and reused many times. They can all record any kind of information – data files, video and TV programmes.

DIVX means digital video express, a new format promoted by the film industry in America. It's like a pay-per-view DVD allowing you to rent or buy a DIVX disk at low price and view its contents within a limited period of time. DIVX players come with a modem which connects to the phone lines to communicate with the central server.

4 ....

The basic pattern is a single-sided, single layer disk with a capacity of 4.7 GB. The single-sided, dual layer disk can hold up to 8.5 GB. The double-sided, single layer disk offers a capacity of 9.4 GB. As the contents are on both sides, the disks must be used in a DVD player capable of reading the two sides. Finally, the double-sided, dual layer disk increases the storage capacity up to 17 GB, with 8.5 GB on each side.

5 ....

There are still too many formats and specifications, but in the near future DVD drives are expected to be compatible with all existing CD and DVD formats. DVDs will gradually replace audio CDs, CD-ROMs and video cassettes.

PC users and movie addicts are waiting with excitement for a universal drive that can play any type of optical disk.

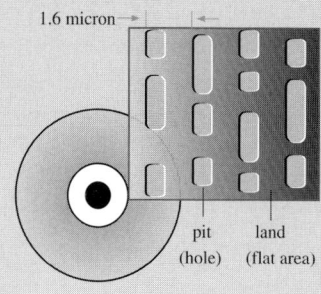

1.6 micron

Close-up of part of a **CD-ROM**.
A CD can hold 650 MB.

pit (hole)   land (flat area)

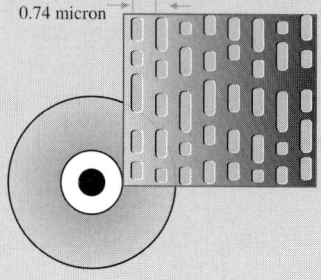

0.74 micron

Close-up of part of a **DVD**.
A basic DVD can hold 4.7 GB.

2 **Read the text again and find:**

1 the compression format used by DVD-video technology
2 two similarities between CDs and DVDs
3 two differences between CDs and DVDs
4 the storage capacity of a basic DVD disk
5 the storage capacity of a double-sided, dual layer DVD

3 **Summarize the technical specifications and uses of these DVD formats.**

DVD-ROM   DVD-R

DVD Video

DIVX   DVD + Rewritable

Discourse: Linking words

4 **Look at paragraph 2 of the text again and put the words in *italics* into one of these columns.**

Addition	Contrast	Result/Effect
....	....	....
....	....	....

5 **Complete these sentences with a linking adverb or conjunction from the list.**

secondly   so   on the other hand
and   while   because of   besides

1 DVD-R disks can record data once, ... DVD+RW disks can be rewritten many times.
2 A DVD+RW drive costs a lot of money, ... you should use it carefully.
3 A DVD-Video can hold a full-length movie in eight different languages .... 32 subtitles.

4 Optical disks can store information at higher densities than magnetic disks. .... , they are not affected by magnetic fields.
5 On the one hand, optical drives offer more storage than hard disks but .... they're slower than hard disks.
6 In the first place, the tracks in a DVD are closer than in a CD, and .... the pits are smaller, so there are more pits per track.
7 IT companies are losing money .... software piracy.

6 **Join the sentences with the words in brackets.**

1 A virus entered the computer. Many files have been destroyed. (*as a result*)
2 DVDs and CDs are physically similar in size. Their data structure is very different. (*although*)
3 Colour, animation and 3D graphics are essential in many applications. They're used in art, graphic design and engineering. (*for example*)
4 In computers, RAM memory is temporary. The ROM section is permanent. (*however*)

Linking words and phrases
- ORDERING points
  First   In the first place   Second   Secondly   Third   Thirdly   Finally
- Indicating ADDITION
  In addition   Besides   Moreover   also   and   Furthermore   What's more
- Making CONTRASTS
  However   although   while   whereas   but   On the one hand ... on the other hand
- Explaining CAUSE or REASON
  For this reason   Owing to this   because of
- Explaining RESULTS
  As a result   so   Thus   Consequently
- Giving EXAMPLES
  For example   For instance   ... such as
- SUMMARY markers
  To sum up   In short   Briefly   In conclusion

Language work: Indefinites

1 **Read the sentences below and underline all the indefinites. Decide whether they act as determiners (accompanying a noun) or pronouns (working as independent items).**

1 Everybody uses Windows.
2 The OS includes all programs which control the basic functions of a PC.
3 We each have a webcam.
4 On each occasion she just missed the train.
5 I've got some books about LINUX.
6 Nobody actually owns the Internet.
7 I've got absolutely nothing to say.
8 There were no messages for you.
9 I had lots of pictures, but none was good enough.

2 **How do you say these two sentences in your language? Is there any difference?**

1 **Every** candidate will be interviewed.
2 **Each** candidate will be interviewed.

3 **Translate these sentences into your language. Do they take a singular or a plural verb?**

1 All are installed.
2 None is/are installed
3 Both are installed.
4 Neither is/are installed.

4 **Use *both*, *neither*, *all* or *none* as in the example.**

Pierre knows how to design Web pages.
Françoise knows how to design Web pages too.
= They both know how to design Web pages.

1 Julio doesn't like this operating system. Lidia doesn't like this operating system either.
.... of them likes/like this operating system.
2 Elena, Jan and Tina have UMTS mobile phones.
They .... have UMTS mobile phones.

3 Floppies, hard disks and Zip drives do not use optical technology.
.... of them uses/use optical technology.
4 Franz and Anna were arrested.
They were .... arrested.

5 **Look at the box. Complete the sentences with *some*, *any*, *somebody*, *something*, *anybody* or *anything*.**

1 .... operating systems occupy a lot of disk space.
2 We can't do .... else.
3 .... will tell you where the Central Bank is.
4 Do you have .... good games?
5 I have a DVD+RW drive. Now I need .... DVDs.
6 If you find .... mistakes, please let me know.
7 Can I get you .... coffee? I've just made some.
8 I can see .... repairing the telephone line.
9 There's .... I want to tell you.
10 I don't have .... plug-in(s) to see this animation.

Universal indefinites

	Determiners	Pronouns
POSITIVE	every	everyone / everybody
	each	everything
	all	each
	both	all
		both
NEGATIVE	no	nobody (no one)
	neither	nothing
		none
		neither

- **Every** and its compounds take a singular verb. *Everybody **needs** somebody to love.*
- **Every** refers to a group.
- **Each** means one by one, considered individually.
- **No** can go with countable and uncountable nouns. *No cigarette is completely harmless. Sorry, I have no time.*

▶

Partitive indefinites

- **Some** and its compounds (*someone, somebody, something*) are used in positive statements.
  Some viruses are transferred via the Web.

  Some is also used when we make an offer or a request, expecting a positive answer.
  Could I have some tea? (request)
  Would you like some biscuits? (offer)

- **Any** and its compounds (*anyone, anybody, anything*) are used in the following cases.

negation	*There aren't any CDs left.*
questions	*Are there any more letters?*
conditional clause	*If you have any doubt, ask her.*

  Any can be used in positive sentences when it means 'it doesn't matter which'.
  Any mobile phone can send SMS messages.

Reading: Computer viruses

6 **Read the text and answer these questions.**

1 What is a computer virus?
2 What are the effects of the *Jerusalem* virus?
3 What type of virus was *Code Red*? How did it spread?
4 What is a Trojan horse?
5 How can viruses enter and infect your computer system?
6 What happened when you opened the attachment of the *ILoveYou* e-mail virus?
7 How can you protect your system from viruses?

7 **Find these words in the text. Then match them with a synonym on the right.**

1	damage	a	activated
2	replicates	b	harm, spoil
3	polymorphic	c	passing through various
4	triggered		stages
5	deleting	d	propagates, extends
6	disguises	e	stop, fail
7	crash	f	erasing
8	spreads	g	masquerades, conceals
		h	creates copies of itself

Computer viruses

A **virus** is a piece of software written deliberately to enter your computer and damage your data. Typically it attaches itself to another program and replicates itself trying to 'infect' as many files as possible. Some viruses are polymorphic (e.g. the *Tequila* mutation). Others are capable of transmitting themselves across the Net.

Here are some types of viruses:

- **Logic bomb** – a virus which is triggered when a specific program is executed. A **time bomb** is activated on a certain day. For example, the *Jerusalem* virus activates on Friday 13th, displaying a black window on the screen and deleting infected files.

- **Macro virus** – it infects documents run by programs that use macros (e.g. word processors). A typical macro virus is *Melissa*, which was passed in MS Word files sent via e-mail.

- **Worm** – a special type of virus that uses computer networks and security holes to reproduce itself independently, without having to attach itself to another program. A worm called *Code Red* replicated itself many times in 2001 infecting thousands of Web servers.

- **Trojan horse** – a destructive program that disguises itself as a safe program. A Trojan horse does not reproduce itself but instead can crash the system or erase the files on your hard drive. The term comes from a Greek legend: the Greeks offered a wooden horse to the Trojans, their enemies. Once the horse was inside the city walls, the Greek soldiers came out of the horse's belly and captured Troy.

Viruses can enter your computer system in three different ways: (i) via a disk drive, when you insert infected disks or CDs; (ii) via files downloaded from the Web, or (iii) via e-mail attachments. When you open an infected file, the virus is activated and installs itself into the computer's memory. Then it spreads to storage devices and may infect your friends' systems through the Net. A good example is *ILoveYou*, an Internet worm released in 2000 as an e-mail attachment (*Love Letter-For-You*). When you opened this file, the virus was sent to everyone in your address book.

But there is protection software (e.g. Norton Anti-virus, McAfee VirusScan) that will help you detect, diagnose and eradicate viruses. Don't forget that new viruses are created every day, so try to update the database of your anti-virus program regularly.

It is a good idea to make a back-up copy of all your important files. It's also advisable not to open e-mails from strangers.

Reading: A virtual interface

1 Read the text opposite and find

1 a type of interface that allows users to select things by clicking on icons and menus
2 the technique which uses a computer model or program to reproduce a particular situation
3 a sort of helmet or goggles that hold the visual and auditory displays
4 a device used to manipulate and move virtual objects with your hands
5 the machines that simulate flying conditions

2 Find the words in the text that correspond to the following.

Paragraph 1
1 artificial reality or environment generated by computers
2 user interface based on virtual reality

Paragraph 2
3 images
4 effect of perceiving a 3-D world by sending two views to the user's right and left eyes

Paragraph 3
5 control device used in video games
6 set of articles of clothing

Paragraph 4
7 displays of things (e.g. works of art)
8 very small

Discourse: Devices for abbreviating

3 Substitute the <u>underlined</u> words with *one*, *ones*, *that*, *there*, *then*, *do so*, or *does*.

1 I met Bill Gates in 1995. I was living in New York <u>in 1995</u>.
2 Ivan likes *The Matrix* film and Sara <u>likes it</u> too.
3 Giving up smoking? Nothing would make me <u>give up smoking</u>.
4 I prefer the sound of a violin to <u>the sound of a trumpet</u>.

5 A: Those glasses that we saw earlier look great.
   B: I don't know which <u>glasses</u> you are talking about.
6 A: I'd like to visit Silicon Valley in the USA.
   B: Why do you want to go <u>to Silicon Valley</u>?
7 A: Which monitor do you want?
   B: Can I have the big <u>monitor</u> please?

Devices for abbreviating

Substitution
This means that one expression is replaced by a shorter word.
- Personal pronouns
  *Peter loves webcams and **he** has two of **them**.*
- Indefinite pronouns
  *The new designs are better than the old **ones**.*
- Adverbs
  *'Let's meet at the cinema.' 'OK. See you **there**.'*
  *'I bought my first computer in 1990.' 'How old were you **then**?'*
- Auxiliary *do*
  *Jo prefers video-conferencing and Marco **does** too.*
- *do / did so*
  *She asked me to check the computer for viruses and I **did so** at once.*

Ellipsis
In ellipsis, part of a sentence is left out. When you omit words, make sure that the sentence remains meaningful.
My video camera, like Maria's ∅, is German.
'Who was playing computer games last night?'
'Marta was ∅.'
If Mr Morgan resigns from the committee, I'm sure that other members will ∅.

Reduced relative clauses
*Do you know the lady **standing** at the door? (= ... who is standing ...)*

Leaving out relative pronouns
We can omit the relative when it's not the subject of the relative clause.
That's the system ∅ I was talking about.

Omitting modifying adverbs
She plays the violin (fairly) well.

Cutting out unnecessary phrases or examples

A *virtual interface*

The most common user interface today is a **graphical user interface** or GUI. Typically, it includes menus, windows, icons, buttons and a mouse as pointing device. But with the development of **virtual reality** (VR) techniques, a different type of interface has emerged: a **virtual interface**. VR uses 3-D graphics and **computer simulation** to generate an **imaginary world** in which the user can move.

In a virtual interface, you put on a **head-mounted display** (HMD) to see the pictures which make you feel as if you are in a 3-D world. Most HMDs have two displays and provide **stereoscopic vision**.

You also use sophisticated **controlling devices** such as 3-D joysticks, gloves, special suits and motion detectors. A **virtual mouse**, trackball or joystick is used to move around the place you are exploring. A **data glove** (or VR glove) has some pressure pads and sensors on the fingers which make you feel as if you are picking up objects and touching things. Full **body suits** with position and bend sensors are used for capturing motion. **Motion detectors** allow the machine to sense when and how you move.

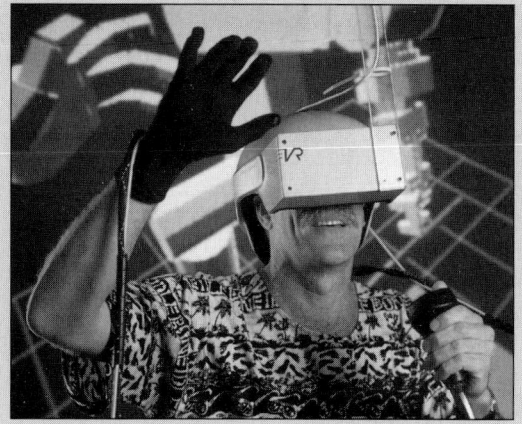

VR systems are already being used in fields like **video games, architectural designs** and **virtual exhibitions**. Other VR applications allow participants to view reality from an advantageous position; for example, **simulators** and **telepresence systems**. Scientists reproduce a particular condition or situation by using a computer program to reproduce it. Pilots use **flight simulators** to do their training. A **telepresence system** connects remote sensors in the real world with the senses of a person; for instance, doctors use tiny cameras and instruments on cables to do complicated surgery; scientists use **remotely operated robots** to work in dangerous conditions, to explore volcanic activity, the ocean depths, or outer space.

VR headsets

Writing: Summarizing

4   **Summarize the text above in 75–80 words. Use devices to abbreviate sentences and focus on important information.**

A virtual interface ... .
....
....
....
....
....
....
....
....
....
....

YOUR DINNER'S VIRTUAL REALITY

PENWILL

Unit 15 *A walk through word processing*

Vocabulary review: Word processors

1 **Look at this screen about computer games.**

   a Translate the menu bar into your own language.

   b Identify the word processing features (in the box) in the text.

> header   footer   bold text   italic text
> web link   underlined text   word count
> margin   inserted picture   selected block
> Times Roman typeface

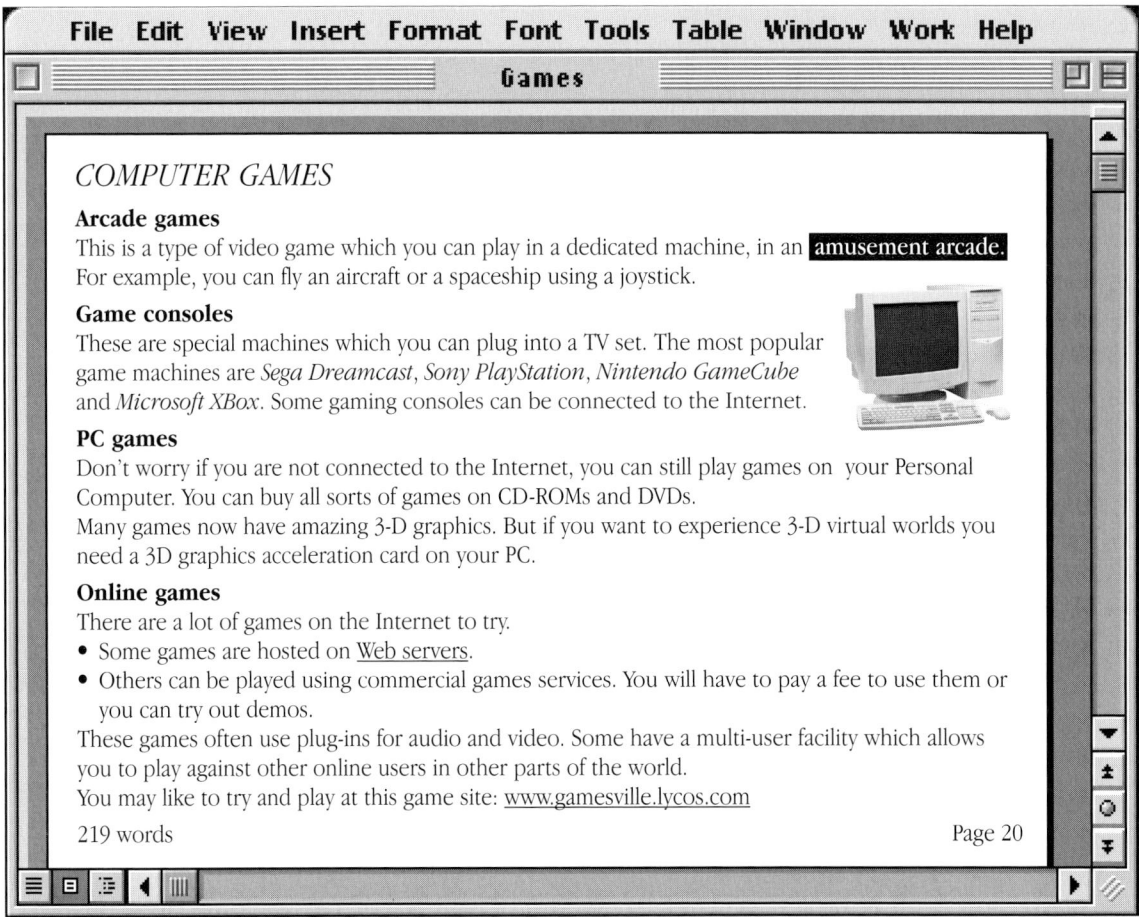

File   Edit   View   Insert   Format   Font   Tools   Table   Window   Work   Help

Games

COMPUTER GAMES

Arcade games
This is a type of video game which you can play in a dedicated machine, in an **amusement arcade.** For example, you can fly an aircraft or a spaceship using a joystick.

Game consoles
These are special machines which you can plug into a TV set. The most popular game machines are *Sega Dreamcast*, *Sony PlayStation*, *Nintendo GameCube* and *Microsoft XBox*. Some gaming consoles can be connected to the Internet.

PC games
Don't worry if you are not connected to the Internet, you can still play games on your Personal Computer. You can buy all sorts of games on CD-ROMs and DVDs.
Many games now have amazing 3-D graphics. But if you want to experience 3-D virtual worlds you need a 3D graphics acceleration card on your PC.

Online games
There are a lot of games on the Internet to try.
• Some games are hosted on <u>Web servers</u>.
• Others can be played using commercial games services. You will have to pay a fee to use them or you can try out demos.
These games often use plug-ins for audio and video. Some have a multi-user facility which allows you to play against other online users in other parts of the world.
You may like to try and play at this game site: <u>www.gamesville.lycos.com</u>

219 words   Page 20

2 **These features are typical in word processing.**
Match them to the correct definition.

1	Search and Replace	a	detects syntax errors
2	Justification	b	can read names and addresses from a database to create personalized letters
3	Hyphenation	c	splits a long word between two lines by a dash '-' or hyphen, so that the text will fit better on the page
4	Mail merge		
5	Spellcheck	d	lines up text on both the left-hand side and the right-hand side
6	Grammar check	e	lets you preset different margins, so you can arrange data in columns
7	Tab function	f	finds words which do not match the program's dictionary and suggests several replacements for the words it doesn't recognize
		g	looks for a particular word phrase in a body of text and lets you change it

Language work: Agreeing and disagreeing

3 **Reply to Sue's comments by agreeing. Use an expression with *so* or *nor/neither*.**

e.g. SUE: *I like computer games.*
YOU: *So do I.*

1 SUE: I can type very fast.
YOU: ....

2 SUE: I don't know how to insert hyperlinks.
YOU: ....

3 SUE: I was at the conference yesterday.
YOU: ....

4 SUE: I'd like to have Microsoft Office XP.
YOU: ....

5 SUE: I didn't choose the right font.
YOU: ....

4 **How would you disagree with Sue's comments?**

e.g. SUE: *I can't speak English.*
YOU: *Oh, I can.*

1 SUE: I'm not interested in computers.
YOU: ....

2 SUE: I saw a UFO last week.
YOU: ....

3 SUE: I still use my old Mac to write letters.
YOU: ....

4 SUE: I've never imported files from a PC to a Mac.
YOU: ....

5 SUE: I won't buy that program.
YOU: ....

Agreeing and disagreeing

To **agree** with an affirmative statement, we use:
so + auxiliary verb + subject

A: *I prefer this word processor.* B: *So do I. (= me too)*

To **agree** with a negative statement, we use:
Nor
Neither + auxiliary verb + subject

A: *He didn't know how to generate a table of contents.*
B: *Nor/Neither did I. (= I didn't know, either)*

To **disagree** with an affirmative statement, we use:
(Oh, / Really?), I + negative auxiliary verb

A: *I could read music when I was 9.*
B: *Oh, I couldn't.*

To **disagree** with a negative statement, we use:
(Oh, / Really?), I + positive auxiliary verb

A: *I love this video game.* B: *Really? I don't.*

Writing: About computer games

5 **Answer this questionnaire.**

> **1** How often do you play computer games?
> ☐ Never ☐ Sometimes ☐ Every day
> ---
> **2** Have you ever played any of these?
> ☐ Game consoles (e.g. PlayStation)
> ☐ PC games
> ☐ Internet games
> ---
> **3** What type of game do you prefer?
> ☐ Adventure
> ☐ Strategy
> ☐ Fantasy sport (football, 3-D car racing, etc.)
> ☐ 3-D action
> ☐ Gambling
> ☐ Educational
> ☐ Board game (chess, monopoly, etc.)
> ---
> **4** What's your favourite computer game?
> ....
> ---
> **5** Can computer games create addiction?
> ☐ Yes ☐ No
> ---
> **6** Is it an expensive hobby?
> ☐ Yes ☐ No
> ---
> **7** Why do you think people enjoy computer games?
> ☐ They're amusing
> ☐ They imply mental challenge
> ☐ You can play games on the Net
> ☐ They're natural; people like competition
> ---
> **8** Why do some people hate computer games?
> ☐ There is no human contact
> ☐ They show violence
> ☐ They create dependence
> ☐ They have negative effects on children

6 **Write a short text about the pros and cons of computer and video games.**

▶

Vocabulary review: What's a spreadsheet?

1 **Solve the clues and complete the crossword.**

1 A spreadsheet program is normally used in b................... for financial planning.
2 It's like a large piece of p................... divided into columns and rows.
3 Each column is labelled with a letter and each r................. is labelled with a number.
4 The point where a column and a row intersect is called a c...................
5 A cell can hold three types of information: text, numbers and f...................
6 You can u................... the information in different worksheets by linking cells.
7 This means that when you make a change in one w................... the same change is made in the other worksheet.
8 Information can be visualized in different ways, such as line g..................., bar or pie charts.
9 Spreadsheet programs are also used to make out i................... and to calculate the VAT of a product.
10 VAT means v................... added tax.
11 Some programs also have a d................... facility which transforms the values in a database. In this case, each column is a field and each row is a record.

Language work: Adverbs

2 **Look at sentences 1–5 and match them with uses a–c.**

1 When you change the value of a cell, the values in other cells are <u>automatically</u> recalculated.
2 A spreadsheet program is <u>quite</u> easy to use.
3 Calculators can do all sorts of calculations. <u>However</u>, they are not so powerful and versatile as spreadsheet programs.
4 Come <u>here,</u> please.
5 They bought *Microsoft Excel* <u>yesterday</u>.

Uses

a Adverbs give information about an action. For example, adverbs of manner, place and time describe how, where or when something happens.
b They modify an adjective or another adverb.
c They connect two sentences (e.g. conjunctive adverbs).

3 **Look at the box first. Decide whether the words in bold in the sentences are adjectives or adverbs.**

1 Marina works **hard** at school.
2 She is a very **hard** worker.
3 This computer is very **fast**.
4 Please don't speak so **fast**.
5 He caught an **early** train.
6 The meeting ended **early**.
7 The mail is delivered **daily**.
8 He keeps up to date with **daily** reports.
9 Don't talk so **loud**.
10 Turn the volume down. That music is very **loud**.
11 She looks **lovely** in that dress.
12 She drives **carefully**.

Adverbs

- In structure, we can distinguish three types of adverbs:
  a simple: *just, only, well, near, down, yet*
  b compounds: *somehow, however*
  c derivational: *quickly, clockwise, eastwards*
- We usually form an adverb of **manner** by adding *-ly* to an adjective.
  e.g. *slow – slowly   possible – possibly*
  Careful! Not all words ending in *-ly* are adverbs.
  For example, these words are adjectives:
  friendly, lovely, lonely, silly, ugly
- Some words have the same form in **adjective** and **adverb** function. Don't confuse them.
  fast, hard, early, late, daily, monthly, loud
  Compare:
  Serge has a **fast** car. (adjective)
  Serge drove **fast**. (adverb)

4   Look at the next box first.
Put the adverbs in the right places.

1 We book our holiday through the Web. (usually)
2 They are fighting. (always)
3 He opens e-mails from strangers. (never)
4 She walks quickly. (home)
5 I have been to London. (often)

5   Rewrite these sentences in the correct order.

1 works / at / Jan / on Saturday mornings / a computer shop
2 We / rugby / see / on TV / rarely / these days
3 will / She / the race / win / probably
4 I ordered / a few / a new computer / ago / weeks

Position of adverbs and adverbial phrases

1 Adverbial phrases which say how, where and when often go in this order:
              manner   place   time
   They danced <u>very well</u> <u>at the concert</u> <u>last night</u>.
2 After verbs of movement, we often put expressions of place first:
              place manner
   Mary went <u>upstairs</u> <u>quietly</u>.
3 Adverbs of frequency (*always, usually, often,* etc.) go before the main verb but after **be** and after the first auxiliary verb.
   Anne-Marie <u>always</u> finishes first.
   Marco is <u>always</u> late.
   He has <u>never</u> surfed the Web.
4 We place adverbs in initial position to show emphasis.
   <u>Usually</u>, Renata doesn't arrive before 8.30.
   <u>Never</u> have I seen such a thing.

Writing: A paperless office?

6   Imagine that you work in a school office which is fully computerized. Write two or three paragraphs about the things that you can do to reduce the cost of paper.

Useful ideas

- use e-mail instead of fax
- prepare the school budget with a spreadsheet program
- scan printed material, then edit it and distribute it in electronic format
- post messages and information on the school website
- publish exercises for students to complete online
- arrange for enrolments for courses to be administered via the website

Vocabulary review: Office software

1 **Can you distinguish these terms? Write a definition for each one.**

   file   record   field

2 **Study this example of a record from a database of students. What fields does it contain?**

DEREHAM SCHOOL
Crown Road, Dereham, Norfolk

Name: Katie Heffernan
Address: 4 Elm Street, Dereham, Norfolk, NR20 4AG
Phone number: 01362 696910
GCSEs: English, Maths, French, Spanish, History, Physics, Biology, Chemistry, Music
Class: 11H
Date of birth: 12/07/1987
Parents: Joe Heffernan Claire Moore
Father's job: Architect
Mother's job: Teacher
Sports: Hockey Netball Swimming

---

3 **What fields would you include in a database for a school library? Try to design a database form.**

4 **Find the type of software in 1–7 used to accomplish each of the office tasks in a–g.**

   1 database
   2 word processor
   3 spreadsheet program
   4 e-mail package
   5 business accounting
   6 video-conferencing
   7 Internet explorer

   a to write letters and faxes
   b to handle accounts and organize wages, taxes, payments, etc.
   c to make calculations in the form of mathematical tables
   d to store, manipulate and retrieve data
   e to exchange messages with clients
   f to search for information on the Web
   g to create virtual meetings over long distances so that the participants can see and hear each other

Writing: A business letter and a fax

5 **Ian Pegg has sent some computer products to one of his clients. Use the phrases from the list to complete the business letter.**

   Yours sincerely
   I am writing
   Dear Ms Atkinson
   We would be grateful if you could
   I am enclosing
   Please contact us

Media Market
Software supplies

58 Merrin Square
Dublin 2
Fax: 1 662 2367
e-mail: soft@mediamarket.com

Ruth Atkinson
38 High Street
Galway

(1) .... ,

(2) .... to confirm that we have sent you 15 laptops and a laser printer, along with Microsoft Access database. Please allow two weeks for delivery.

(3) .... two copies of commercial invoices. (4) .... make your payment by cheque or directly to our bank account through the Internet.

We are delighted to inform you that we are offering our clients an online course on 'A paperless office', free of charge.

(5) .... if you require any further information or explanation.

(6) .... ,

Ian Pegg
Assistant Manager

---

6 Imagine you are Ruth Atkinson. When you try to use the laser printer, it gives continuous error messages and the database program can't be installed. Write a fax complaining about this and asking for a new printer and an upgraded version of the database.

FAX MESSAGE

Date: ....
TO: Media Market Software supplies
Fax: 1 662 2367
FROM: Ruth Atkinson

Dear Mr Pegg,

....
....
....
....
....
....
....
....
....

Number of pages: 1
Please call if you experience any transmission problems.

Language work: Number and case

7 Write the plural of these words.

1 database	6 technology	11 thief
2 business	7 address	12 toy
3 facility	8 tax	13 physics
4 software	9 medium	14 belief
5 salary	10 hero	15 switch

8 Look at the box. Use the possessive *'s* or the structure with *of* to indicate possession.

1 Jack + his briefcase
2 Russia + its influence
3 the Internet + its influence
4 yesterday + its news
5 Parliament + its Houses
6 mountain + its top

9 Right or wrong? Tick (✓) the correct sentences and rewrite the incorrect ones.

1 This is Melita's file, isn't it?
2 I bought this software package at Stanley's.

3 It's the minidisk player of Kelly.
4 We're having dinner at Samson's at 8 pm.
5 Have you seen the girls's Nintendo GameCube?
6 What do you think of the idea of Peter?
7 This is Fatima's computer.
8 These are the CDs of my brother.

Nouns: number and case
Plurals See page 79 in the Student's Book.

Possessive *'s*
The possessive *'s* is used when the first noun is the name of a person, group of people, organization, country or animal. It's also called the genitive case.
e.g. *the boy's bike (= The bike belongs to the boy.)*
Follow these rules:
* Singular noun + *'s*
  the company's structure
* Plural noun + *'*
  my cousins' computer
* Irregular plural noun + *'s*
  the children's PlayStation

We also use the genitive *'s* with expressions of measurement of **time** and time 'when'.
today's paper   two hours' delay

Independent genitive
This occurs when we omit the item referring to homes or businesses.
I spent the night at Julia's. (= at Julia's house)
I hate going to the dentist's. (= to the dentist's surgery)

In other cases we generally prefer the **of** construction.
the structure of plastic   the leg of the table

Unit 18 *Faces of the Internet*

Vocabulary review: The Net

1 **Complete the sentences with a term from the list. Then write the words in the crossword.**

> modem password online download
> Telnet hyperlink Web protocol

1 When you are connected to the Internet you are described as being ....

2 A .... is a piece of text or an image that, when selected, takes you to other Internet sites.

3 The Internet is based on a .... called TCP/IP.

4 You need a .... to convert computer data into a form that can be transmitted over the phone lines.

5 Users have to enter the log-in name and a .... to gain access to the Net.

6 FTP software allows you to .... files from the Net to your computer.

7 The World Wide Web is known as the ....

8 To 'log on' to a remote computer you need to run a .... program.

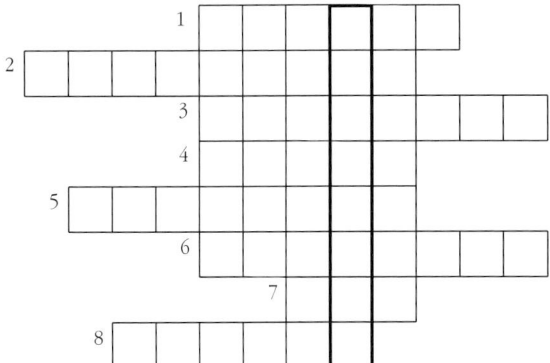

Writing: An e-mail

2 **It is your best friend's birthday and you're going to have a surprise party for him. Complete this e-mail to one of your friends about your plans.**

You may like to use some expressions from the box.

> buy a book
> bring some music CDs
> send a virtual present
> make sandwiches
> choose a nice movie on DVD
> bring some drinks
> give him/her a free subscription to a digital TV
> invite friends and classmates

File Edit Mailbox Message Transfer Special Window

robken@hotmail.com

Send

Robert,

It's Phil's birthday on Saturday and I'd like to arrange a surprise party for him. Can you please help me organize everything?
I'm going to ....
Phil likes reading very much. Shall we ....
.... ?
I'd also like to ....
But I can't ....
Could you ....
.... and .... ?
Please don't forget to ....

Give me a ring tomorrow, OK?
Liz

Language work: Questions

3 **Look at the answers 1–8 and make a question about Peter Morgan for each answer.**

1 Peter Morgan is <u>35 years old</u>.
2 He lives <u>in London</u>.
3 He works <u>as an online researcher</u>.
4 He uses the Internet <u>to find information requested by clients</u>.
5 He wrote a book on e-commerce <u>in 2001</u>.
6 He finishes work <u>at 5 pm</u>.
7 In his free time, he likes <u>going to the movies and meeting friends</u>.
8 He goes to the cinema <u>twice a month</u>.

4 **You are going to carry out a survey about the use of the Internet at your school/work.**

Prepare the questionnaire. You can use these expressions to help you write the questions.

e.g. *What type of modem do you have?*

favourite Internet portal
kind of information you get on the Web
number of e-mail addresses you have
have an anti-virus program
send instant messages to friends
ever played games online
ever bought things over the Net
ever booked your holiday on the Net
safe to shop on the Internet
use mobile phone or PDA to access the Net
ever download electronic music
know how to compress and decompress files
create and design own Web pages

Questions

> Can I join the school mailing list?

> Do you have a nickname on the Web?

> What does FTP mean?

> How fast is an ADSL modem?

In questions, we normally place the auxiliary verb before the subject. If there is no other auxiliary, we use **do/does** or **did**.

Wh-questions

* They begin with a question word (*who, whose, what, which, when, where, how, why*).
  When *is your birthday?*
* When *who, what*, or *which* is the subject, it comes directly before the verb.
  Who put that on my desk? (NOT ~~Who did put ...?~~)
* Unlike yes-no questions, wh-questions generally have **falling** intonation.

  Where do you LIVE?

Question words

People	**Who** *opened this letter?*
	Whose *is this bike?*
	Which *one is your boyfriend?*
Things	**What** *did she give you?*
	Which *is your book? The blue one.*
Place	**Where** *is my dictionary?*
Time	**When** *did you meet her?*
	How long *have you been waiting?*
	How often *do you chat online?*
	What time *do you start work?*
Reason	**Why** *did you arrive late?*
Quantity	**How many** *CDs do you want?*
	How much *does a modem cost?*
Manner	**How** *do you compress a file?*
Means	**How** *shall we go, by bus or by train?*
Others	**How tall** *is she?*
	How long/deep *is the pool?*
	How fast *is this Pentium chip?*
	How old *is the President?*

Unit 19 *Graphics and design*

Vocabulary review: Graphics software

1 Complete the sentences with a term from the list. Then write the words in the crossword.

> pixel   icons   images   shading   designer   interface   palette   graphs

1 Graphic .... let us visualize the effects of the PC's processor on our work.
2 A good user .... often uses windows, pop-up menus and graphics to make communication with machines easier.
3 The total number of colours available is called the colour ....
4 Business people present information visually in .... and diagrams.
5 Rendering techniques are used to make the image look realistic. They include ...., light sources and reflections.
6 Each dot on the screen is called a picture element or ....
7 We use visual symbols or .... to represent objects or tasks.
8 A Web page .... uses pictures, image maps and animation to make pages more effective.

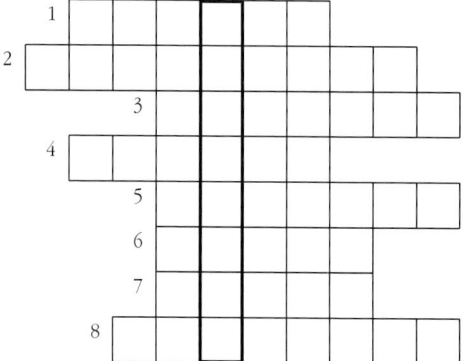

Language work: The *-ing* form

2 Look at the box. Identify the *-ing* forms and decide whether they are a gerund, a present participle or an adjective.

1 Computer animation is the process of creating objects which move across the screen.
2 The lady carrying the books is the deputy head.
3 Climbing that mountain was exhausting.
4 A WAN is a network linking nodes over long distances.
5 She was printing the report.
6 Newspapers are full of depressing news nowadays.
7 Advertising on the web is becoming fashionable.

3 Fill in the blanks with a suitable gerund.

1 Have you finished .... yet?
2 That film is not worth ....
3 I'm thinking of .... a webcam.
4 I look forward to .... from you soon.
5 My best friend enjoys ....
6 I don't mind ....
7 Sarah can't imagine .... abroad. She is very happy in England.

The *-ing* form

The *-ing* form appears in three different constructions. Don't confuse them.
1 ***Smoking*** *is bad for your health.*
2 *'What are you **doing**?' 'We are **searching** for information about the Beatles.'*
3 *This video game is very **exciting**.*

In 1, *smoking* is a **gerund** acting as the subject of the sentence. A **gerund** refers to an activity or process.
In 2, *doing* and *searching* are **present participles**. This form is used in:
• progressive tenses
• reduced relative clauses

▶

*The girl **writing** on the board is very clever. (= who is writing ...)*
In 3, *exciting* is an **adjective**.

Uses of the gerund
A gerund can be used in the following ways:
a As the subject of a verb
  *Text **handling** and DTP **publishing** have improved in the last few years.*
b As the complement of the subject
  *My favourite hobby is **skiing**.*
c As the object of a verb
  *I have never done any **programming** in Java.*
d As the object of a preposition
  *CAD programs are widely used **in engineering**.*
e As the complement of a verb
  *I like **reading** magazines about computers.*
  Some verbs are followed by the *-ing* form, not by the infinitive. Here are the most common:

avoid	give up	look forward to
deny	hate	mind
enjoy	imagine	postpone
fancy	involve	resist
finish	keep	suggest

f After certain expressions

it's no use	it's not worth
can't stand	can't help
get used to	be used to
there's no point in	

4 **Complete these sentences with the *-ing* form of an appropriate verb from the list.**

do	protest	scale	test
visit	perform	laugh	spend

1 She had to postpone .... her homework. She felt ill.
2 He likes .... Internet music sites.
3 It's no use .... It won't help much.
4 I can't help .... at it.
5 .... is making an object larger or smaller.
6 There is no point in .... all that money.
7 PCs generate graphics by .... mathematical calculations on data.
8 A lot of time and money are saved by .... a car design before making the product.

Writing: About you

5 **Look at the box. Use the *-ing* form or the infinitive. Write about something that you ...**

- have stopped doing
- must remember to do
- remember doing when you were a child
- would like to do
- can't stand doing
- are used to doing
- like doing

I have stopped ...

Changes in meaning
Some verbs take *to*-infinitive or *-ing* form with a change in meaning:

forget + to-infinitive = not remember
I'm sorry, I forgot to post the letter.
forget + *-ing* form = forget a past action
I'll never forget flying over Canada.

remember + to-infinitive = remember to do
Remember to turn off the PC.
remember + *-ing* form = recall a past action
She doesn't remember driving that night.

stop + to-infinitive = pause temporarily
They stopped to send a fax.
stop + *-ing* form = finish
They stopped sending faxes.

need + to-infinitive = it's necessary
She needs to work harder.
need + *-ing* form = passive meaning
The monitor needs repairing. (= to be repaired)

"During the time you've been creating the computer model, we've built it."

Unit 20 *Desktop publishing*

Vocabulary review: DTP software

1 Complete the sentences with these words.

> service bureau   font   imagesetters
> import   clip art   layout   desktop

1 A .... publishing system lets you create high-quality publications.

2 A page .... application enables you to format pages of text and graphics; it involves specifying fonts, columns, text styles, kerning, etc.

3 The term '..................' refers to the shape, style and size of a typeface, e.g. **Times Bold at 10pt**.

4 During the creation of a DTP document you can .... text, tables, graphics, and scanned photos from other programs and put them on your page.

5 The collections of images inserted to illustrate brochures, flyers, posters, etc. are called '..................'.

6 A .... is a company that specializes in desktop publishing services.

7 Desktop publishers use .... to generate high-resolution output on paper or film.

Reading: Steps in a DTP publication

2 The creation of a DTP document involves various phases. Put these steps in the correct order.

e.g. *1a*

a First the DTP designer decides on the basic form of the document (type of document, general design, colour, fonts, images required, etc.).

b The last step is to take the files to a service bureau and print the publication on an imagesetter.

c To create a DTP document, the designer begins by selecting a template or by specifying the settings of a new document (page size, margins, columns, paragraph styles, master pages, etc.).

d After the text is edited, the designer imports the pictures and uses precise tools to position, scale, crop and rotate all the items.

e The next step is to type the text directly or to import it from a word processing program like MS Word or WordPerfect.

f Once the file is composed and saved, the designer has to prepare it for printing, which involves verifying the colour specification, creating a PostScript or PDF file, exporting the file in HTML format for the Web, doing proofs, etc.

3 Look at this page designed with a DTP package.

a ....   e ....   f ....

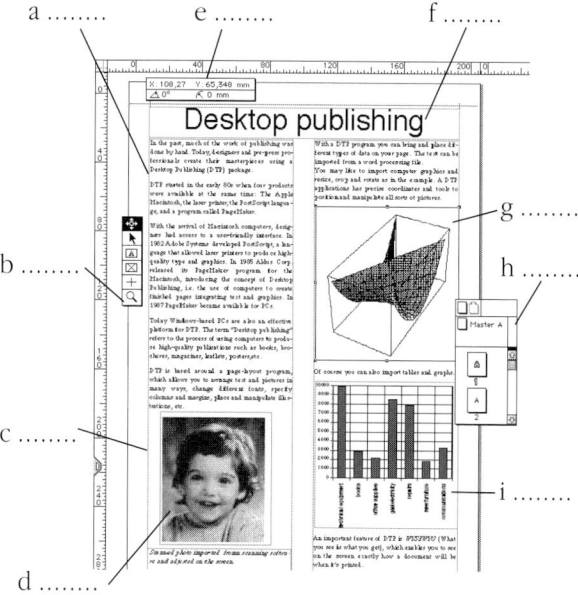

a Identify the types of data imported into the DTP software.

1 text
2 scanned photo
3 bar chart
4 graphic

b Find these tools.

5 toolbox

6 layout of master pages

7 dimensions

8 guide

9 headline box

c Write your own definition of 'desktop publishing'.

Word building: Making new words

4 Look at these words and decide:
- which process of word formation has been applied
- what part of speech each word is (noun, verb, adjective or adverb)

print (base)

1 printer	4 printed	7 imprint
2 reprint	5 print-out	8 printing
3 printable	6 blueprint	9 footprint

Word formation
New words are formed in three main ways:

1 Affixation
- adding a prefix to the base:
  *operate – **co**operate*
- adding a suffix to the base:
  *free – free**dom***

2 Conversion, i.e. assigning one class to another:
drive (verb) – drive (noun)

3 Compounding, i.e. adding one base to another:
key + board = keyboard

Language work: Order of adjectives

5 Look at the box below. Rewrite each description in the correct order.

e.g. programmer: young   a   clever   computer
a clever young computer programmer

1 software: mail   electronic

2 company: computer   personal   a   hardware

3 industry: mobile   phone   a

4 application: layout   page   a

5 car: luxurious   British   a   modern

6 jeans: blue   fashionable   Italian

7 shirt: polyester   blue   a

8 film: detective   a   new   French

9 man: French   attractive   an   old

Order of adjectives before the noun
The rules are a bit complex and there are also exceptions, but this is the usual order:

opinion	description	colour	nationality	material	purpose	headword
attractive		blue	Italian	nylon	swimming	**suits**
a nice	new		Japanese		computer	**shop**

NOTES
- Adjectives are ordered from most **subjective** (e.g. *nice*) to most **objective** (e.g. *metal*).
- **Opinions** often come before **descriptions** (how big? + how old? + what shape?).
- It is not common for a noun to be described by more than three adjectives.

Unit 21 *Web design*

Language work: Modal verbs 2

1 Look at the box. Ask for permission to do these things. Use *can*, *may* or *could*.

1 use the phone at a friend's house
2 read someone's newspaper; you are on a train
3 park your car in someone else's garage
4 send a fax from someone's house
5 ask a question at a business meeting

2 Can you lend me £5? Imagine you are in class. Use *can* or *will* to make requests. If you want to be more polite or formal (e.g. because the request is unusual) use *could*, *would you (mind)* ...

Requests
1 open the window
2 switch on the heater
3 put a music CD on
4 pass a dictionary to you
5 speak louder

3 Change these orders into requests.

1 Stop smoking – it's not allowed here.
   ....
2 Send me a catalogue of your products.
   ....
3 Translate this web page for me.
   ....
4 Lend me some money.
   ....
5 Give me the password.
   ....

4 Read this text and then match the modal verbs (1–5) with the correct meaning (a–c).

We are sending two students to a course on web design next week, so they won't come into college.

The course could be beneficial for all of us. They may well learn HTML and Java. From what I've heard, it should be interesting. One thing is sure: it will be expensive.

1 They won't come
2 The course could be beneficial
3 They may learn
4 It should be interesting
5 It will be expensive

a It is possible that ...
b It's certain that ...
c It's probable (likely) to happen

5 Complete these sentences with *can, could, was able to, must* or *can't*.

1 Sue .... draw and paint very well.
2 In spite of the difficulties, he .... to repair the hard disk.
3 I .... play the guitar when I was 7.
4 That news report .... be true. It's impossible.
5 She can speak seven foreign languages. She .... be very clever.

Modal Verbs 2

Permission

- In informal situations (speaking to friends or people we know well), we use **can**.
  Can I use your computer?
- In formal situations, we use **may**.
  May I use your computer?
- We use **could** if we want to be polite. **Could** is less formal than **may**.
  Could I use your computer?

Requests

Informal: *Can you turn up the radio, please?*
Neutral: *Will you turn up the radio, please?*
More formal and polite:
  Could you turn up the radio, please?
  Would you turn up the radio, please?
  Would you mind turning up the radio, please?

Ability

- We use **can** in the present and **could** in the past.
  *She **can** type very fast.*
  *She **could** swim when she was 5.*
  Can borrows the rest of its tenses from **be able to**.
  *Jess **hasn't been able to** get a job yet.*
  *He **won't be able to** attend the meeting next week.*

▶

- We use **was able to** or **could** to express ability for repeated actions in the past.
  *He **could/was able to** surf the web when he was 8.*
- For a single particular achievement in the past we use **was able to**.
  *His English wasn't very good, but he **was able to** understand most of the film. (= managed to ...)*

Deduction

- We use **must** when we are sure about something or we think it's logically probable. We use **can't** when it's logically improbable.
  Someone is knocking at the door.
  A: *It **must** be Alex. He said he might come.*
  B: *It **can't** be Alex. It's too early.*

Here are some popular web page editors:

- Dreamweaver (Macromedia)
  http://www.macromedia.com
- FrontPage (Microsoft)
  http://www.microsoft.com/frontpage
- HotDog (Sausage software)
  http://www.sausage.com/
- Netscape Composer (part of Communicator)
  http://www.netscape.com/

Writing: A web page

6 **Design and create a web page about your city, town or village. You can use the document below as a model.**

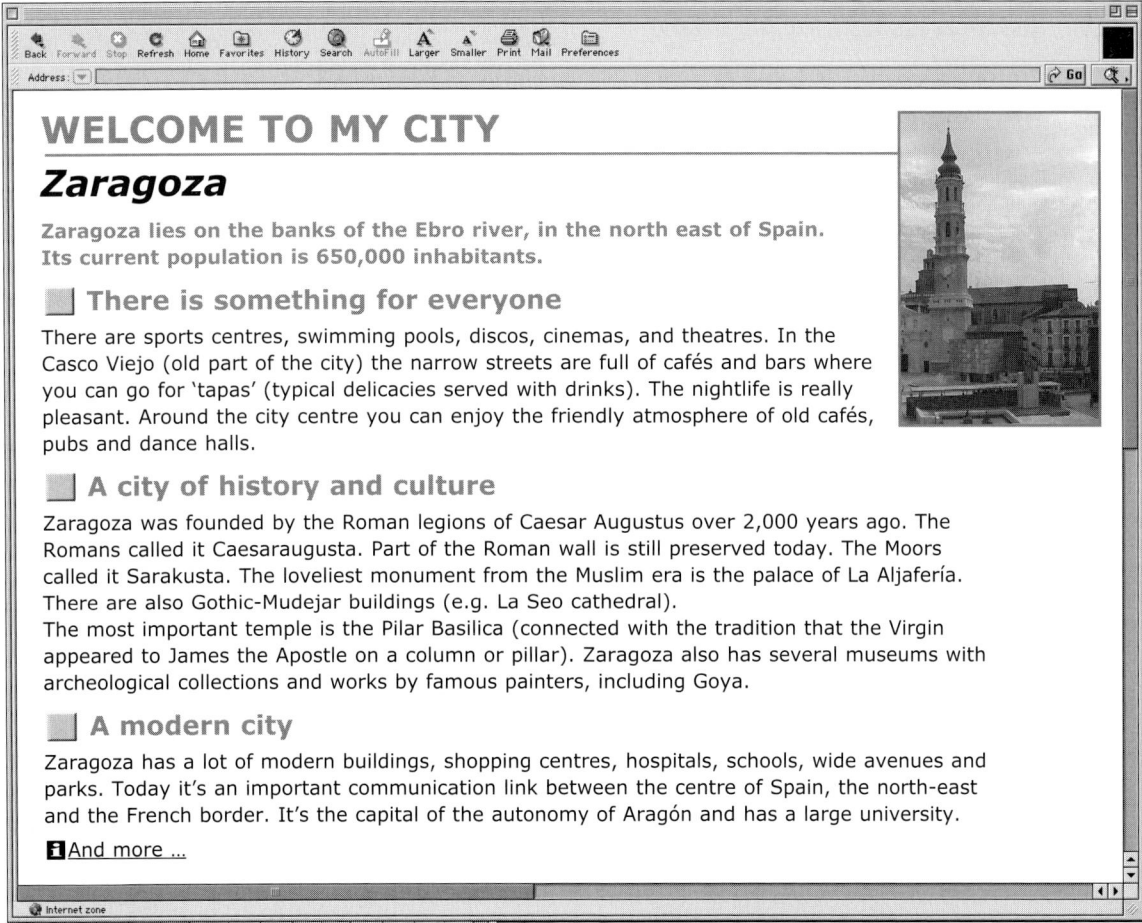

WELCOME TO MY CITY

Zaragoza

Zaragoza lies on the banks of the Ebro river, in the north east of Spain. Its current population is 650,000 inhabitants.

There is something for everyone

There are sports centres, swimming pools, discos, cinemas, and theatres. In the Casco Viejo (old part of the city) the narrow streets are full of cafés and bars where you can go for 'tapas' (typical delicacies served with drinks). The nightlife is really pleasant. Around the city centre you can enjoy the friendly atmosphere of old cafés, pubs and dance halls.

A city of history and culture

Zaragoza was founded by the Roman legions of Caesar Augustus over 2,000 years ago. The Romans called it Caesaraugusta. Part of the Roman wall is still preserved today. The Moors called it Sarakusta. The loveliest monument from the Muslim era is the palace of La Aljafería. There are also Gothic-Mudejar buildings (e.g. La Seo cathedral).
The most important temple is the Pilar Basilica (connected with the tradition that the Virgin appeared to James the Apostle on a column or pillar). Zaragoza also has several museums with archeological collections and works by famous painters, including Goya.

A modern city

Zaragoza has a lot of modern buildings, shopping centres, hospitals, schools, wide avenues and parks. Today it's an important communication link between the centre of Spain, the north-east and the French border. It's the capital of the autonomy of Aragón and has a large university.

And more ...

Unit 22 *Multimedia*

Vocabulary review: Multimedia systems

1 Solve the clues and complete the puzzle.

1 The most common graphics .... on the Web are .gif and .jpg.

2 To capture sounds in a digital format and play them back, modern PCs contain a .... card.

3 Compressed music files can be played with an MP3 ....

4 Most multimedia software is distributed on .... disks (e.g. CD-ROM, DVD).

5 MIDI stands for .... Instrument Digital Interface.

6 The term 'computer ....' refers to drawings that have moving images.

7 Text with links which take you to other Web pages.

8 DVDs will eventually replace .... tapes.

9 To make a movie on your PC you need a special video .... program.

10 Concerts and other events are broadcast over the Web in a process called '...................'.

Reading: MP3 music

2 Read the text and find answers to these questions.

1 What is MP3?

2 Why is MP3 technology so popular?

3 What software do you need to expand and play MP3 music files?

4 What is streaming audio?

5 How can you make your own MP3s?

6 Why are music companies so angry about the MP3 format?

Music for an electronic generation

MP3 technology has revolutionized the music industry. It's a standard format that compresses audio files enabling them to be transmitted over the Net much more easily. This also makes them easier to download, attach to an e-mail or store on disk. It means you can listen to music at high-quality sound for little or no cost.

You can use MP3 music in two main ways:

• You can expand and play MP3 files by using an MP3 player, which you can download from the Internet. Two popular choices are *Winamp* (from Nullsoft) and *RealJukebox* (from RealNetworks). They support streaming MP3 music, which lets you play a file while it's downloading.

• You can also create your own MP3 files from your CDs. You can do this using a CD ripper, a program that extracts music tracks and saves them on disk. Then using an encoder they're converted into the MP3 format. A program like *MusicMatch* has all that you need to turn CD tracks straight into MP3 song files.

To find MP3 music titles on the Web you need an MP3 search engine, or you can visit music portal sites like MP3.com and Emusic.com.

You can play MP3 music on your PC, or you can use a portable MP3 player. This looks like a personal stereo, but instead of CDs it uses a memory card.

A problem with MP3 music is that a lot of files are pirated and offered free on illegal websites.

Big record companies are angry about this because they may lose a lot of money. For this reason, they are taking initiatives to protect digital music from piracy.

The puzzle grid spells MULTIMEDIA vertically.

3 **Match each word 1–8 with its partner a–h to make a common technical term.**

1	compression	a	speaker
2	sound	b	company
3	web	c	engine
4	record	d	attachment
5	search	e	site
6	stereo	f	protection
7	e-mail	g	format
8	copyright	h	card

4 **Which verbs on the left are frequently found with nouns on the right?**

1	to download	a	the Web
2	to install	b	files
3	to compose	c	software
4	to browse	d	data
5	to process	e	music

Language work: Adverbial clauses

5 **Look at the box. Underline the subordinate clauses below and decide what type of meaning they convey.**

e.g. *Send me an SMS <u>as soon as you arrive at the airport</u>.* = *Time*

1 It was so cold that the water froze. = ...
2 Teachers use multimedia software to teach subjects like music and languages. = ...
3 Put the CDs wherever you like. = ...
4 If you bring your digital video camera, we can make a movie on my PC. = ...
5 Even though she has lived in Boston for three years, she can't speak English. = ...
6 As it was late, we decided to leave. = ...

6 **Rewrite these sentences. Keep the same meaning.**

1 Paul Scott is very famous but he is unhappy.
Although ....
2 Her computer doesn't work properly, so she has decided to format the hard disk.
As ....
3 He can't buy a multimedia PC because he has no money.
Since ....
4 She'll buy a new PC when she gets paid.
As soon as ....
5 He'll go to a computer shop, but he'll look at a brochure first.
Before ....
6 The Internet won't expand if there isn't a good telephone system.
Unless ....

Adverbial clauses
They express circumstances (time, reason, etc.).

Time
Introduced by *when, as soon as, until, before, since, while, after.*
*I'll phone **when** he arrives home.*

Place
Introduced by *where* and *wherever.*
*The reporter walked **where** the bomb had exploded.*

Concession
Introduced by *although, even though, whereas.*
*Some kids like classical music **whereas** others hate it.*

Reason/Cause
Introduced by *because, since, as.*
***Since** it was raining, we stayed at home.*

Result
Introduced by *so ... that, such ... that, so.*
*He was **such** a good teacher **that** everyone liked him.*

Purpose
Introduced by *to, in order to, so as to* + infinitive.
*Turn the radio down **so as not to** wake the baby.*

Condition
Introduced by *if, unless, as long as, provided that.*
*I'll type the report **if** you lend me your laptop.*

• **Remember!** *Unless* means *if not.*
*You can't use this PC **if** you **don't** know the entry password. (= ... **unless** you know ...)*

Unit 23 *Program design*

Word search: Programming

1 Find 10 words about 'programming'.

F	H	C	G	Y	B	U	G	S	F	R
L	S	O	I	R	A	H	M	E	A	E
O	R	M	G	R	S	M	C	Z	D	P
W	L	P	X	Y	I	O	M	O	C	A
C	P	I	G	R	C	M	C	F	A	S
H	R	L	S	S	A	O	M	E	L	C
A	C	E	G	P	A	M	B	L	Z	A
R	D	R	G	R	A	Q	M	O	R	L
T	C	O	I	E	A	M	C	U	L	G
O	R	T	D	E	B	U	G	G	E	R
P	R	O	G	R	A	M	M	E	R	O

Reading: Programming steps

2 These words are missing from the text. Decide where they fit.

> errors program compiled debugging
> flowchart documentation language

Programming steps

To write a (1) ...., software engineers usually follow these steps:

First they try to understand the problem and define the purpose of the program.

Next they design a step-by-step plan of instructions. This usually takes the form of a (2) ...., a diagram that uses standardized symbols showing the logical relationship between the various parts of the program.

These logical steps are then translated into instructions written in a high-level computer (3) .... (PASCAL, COBOL, C++, etc.). These computer instructions are called the 'source code'. The program is then (4) ...., a process that converts the source code into machine code (binary code), the language that computers understand.

Testing programs are then run to detect (5) .... in the program. Errors are known as 'bugs', and the process of correcting these errors is called (6) '....................'. Engineers must find the origin of each error, then write the correct instruction, compile the program again, and conduct another series of tests. Debugging continues until the program runs smoothly.

Finally, software developers write detailed (7) .... for the users. Manuals tell us how to use programs like word processors, databases or Web browsers.

3 Refer to the text again and answer these questions.

1 What is a flowchart?
2 What type of language is used by software developers when they write source code?
3 What is 'debugging' a program?

Language work: The infinitive

4 What follows? Infinitive (with or without *to*) or the *-ing* form?
Look at the box opposite and complete these sentences using the correct form of these verbs.

spend	do	meet	understand
live	buy	remove	

1 We had arranged .... in my office to discuss the problem.
2 I don't really fancy .... my holidays with my parents.
3 He refuses .... the project with me.
4 The only language computers can .... directly is called 'machine code'.
5 A debugger is a tool which helps programmers .... errors or ' bugs' from a program.
6 Can you imagine .... without robots and computers?
7 I simply can't afford .... a new car.

5 Choose the correct answer.

1 I'm not interested in .... that computer language.
   a learn   b learning   c to learn
2 You promised not .... anybody my secret.
   a tell   b telling   c to tell
3 I can't get used .... a voice recognition system.
   a use   b to using   c to use
4 I would prefer .... by train.
   a travel   b travelling   c to travel

5 I would rather .... the small one
   than the large one.
   a have   b having   c to have
6 Would you mind .... the window?
   a open   b opening   c to open
7 They may not .... to the conference.
   a come   b coming   c to come
8 Can you make this old PC .... ?
   a start   b starting   c to start

**6 Complete the sentences describing each
    picture. Use infinitives.**

1 e.g. *Franz helped
   his mother carry the
   books.*

2 The manager
   reminded Freya ....

   ....

3 Ludwig invited Pedro

   ....

   ....

4 The pilot asked the
   passengers ....

   ....

5 The teacher ordered

   ....

   ....

6 Eva advised Marta ....

   ....

   ....

7 The bank robbers
   told ....

   ....

8 The engineer warned
   the employees ....

   because ....

The use of the infinitive

The **to-infinitive** is used:

a to express purpose:
   *In a flowchart, special symbols are used **to
   indicate** different functions.*
   *I went to England **to learn** English.* (NOT ... ~~for
   to learn~~)

b as the complement of adjectives and nouns:
   *I'm **pleased to meet** you.*
   *The HTML language is **easy to use**.*

c after adjectives or adverbs accompanied by **too**
   or **enough**:
   *This program runs **too slowly to do** the
   simulation.* (**too** + adj. or adverb)
   *She is not **old enough to do** this.* (adj. + **enough**)

d as the complement of certain verbs:
   • Verb + infinitive. Here are the most common
     verbs:

afford	decide	manage
agree	demand	offer
appear	expect	plan
arrange	fail	promise
ask	hope	refuse
attempt	learn	try

   *I can't afford **to buy** a laser printer.*
   *Experts are trying **to develop** better programs.*

   • Verb + object + infinitive. Here are the most
     common verbs:

advise	expect	recommend
allow	force	remind
ask	help	teach
beg	invite	tell
enable	order	want
encourage	persuade	warn

   *The program documentation enables the **user
   to operate** the program correctly.*
   *A lightpen allows the user **to draw** on the screen.*

The **bare infinitive** (without **to**) is used:

a after modal auxiliary verbs: *can, could, may,
   might, will, would, shall, should, would rather*
   *Unfortunately, computers can't **understand**
   English.*
   *I'd rather **buy** a game than a spreadsheet program.*

b after the verbs **make** and **let**
   *Instructions make a PC **perform** a specified task.*
   *Let me **show** you how this program works.*

NOTE
In the passive form we use the **to-infinitive**:
*She was made **to apologize**.*

Language work: Passive forms

1 Underline the passive verbs in this text. How do we form the passive?

MORNING NEWS

3rd March

A HACKER has been sent to jail for fraudulent use of credit card numbers. Nicholas Cook, 26, was arrested by police officers near a bank cash point last month.

Eight months earlier, he had been caught as he was copying hundreds of computer programs illegally. After an official inquiry, he was accused of software piracy and he was fined £2,000.

Three months ago he was charged with breaking into computer systems just for fun. He also admitted he had infected a company network with a new virus. On that occasion he was released on bail.

It is reported that in the last few years he has been using 'sniffer' programs to obtain crucial data from bank accounts. Cook is the first person sentenced to two years in prison for stealing passwords and getting money by credit card fraud.

Government officials say that new anti-hacking legislation will be introduced in the EU next year.

2 Read the text again. Find examples of the passive in these tenses:

Past simple: ....

Present perfect: ....

Past perfect: ....

Will future: ....

3 Complete the sentences using the correct past simple passive of these verbs.

write	invent	print	build
discover	broadcast	use	paint

1 The pyramids .... by the Ancient Egyptians.
2 The first western books .... by Johannes Gutenberg in the 15th century.
3 Hamlet .... by William Shakespeare.
4 The telephone .... in the USA in 1876 by Alexander Graham Bell.
5 Radio waves .... in 1887 by Heinrich Hertz.
6 The first TV programme .... in 1925.
7 A computer .... as a word processor in 1964.
8 *Guernica* .... by Pablo Picasso.

The passive

The subject of a passive verb corresponds to the object of an active verb.

Active voice: Intel **makes** Pentium chips.

Passive voice: Pentium chips **are made** by Intel.

Present simple	This engine **is made** in Korea.
Present progressive	PCs **are** constantly **being improved**.
Past simple	BASIC **was devised** in 1964.
Past progressive	My printer **was being repaired**, so I couldn't print out the report.
Present perfect	A supercomputer **has been developed** by IBM.
Past perfect	The system **had been infected** by a new virus.
Future simple	Our society **will be controlled** by intelligent machines.
Future perfect	By the year 2020, teachers **will have been replaced** by robots.
Modal verbs	Computers **may** also **be connected** via satellite.
Infinitive	A modem permits digital data **to be converted** into sound signals.

NOTES

- When we mention the agent we use **by**.
  Computer languages are designed by software developers.
- We omit the agent when we don't know its identity or it is obvious.
  The PCs were stolen last night.
- We often use the passive to give an objective tone in technical writing.
  Data is lost when the PC is turned off.
- 'Get' can be used with the passive in informal English.
  *The hard disk **got damaged**.*

4 Complete the text with the correct passive form.

How chips are made

Inside computers, the CPU is a microprocessor chip. Most processors (1) (make) .... of silicon. This material can be obtained from beach sand and works well because it's a semiconductor of electricity.

Manufacturers make large crystals of high-quality silicon and then each crystal (2) (cut) .... into slices less than a millimetre thick. These slices, called wafers, (3) (treat) .... with chemicals, gases and light before they are cut into individual chips.

In the next step, millions of transistors and very small wires (4) (build) .... onto the chip in several layers.

After this, the chip (5) (test) .... many times to ensure that all switches and circuits work correctly.

Finally, each chip (6) (insert) .... into a protective package, which allows the processor to connect to other devices on the motherboard of the computer.

5 Mixed tenses
Complete these sentences with a suitable passive verb.

1 Delphi (often use) .... for general purpose programs.
2 C (develop) .... in the 1970s to support the UNIX operating system.
3 These microchips (make) .... in Japan.
4 Sorry about the mess – the machines (replace) ....
5 New languages on Artificial Intelligence (must develop) ....
6 A serious error (just find) .... in this program.
7 In the near future, the Internet and other IT devices (introduce) .... into cars.

Writing: How a car is made

6 The diagram explains how a car is made. Continue the description of the process. Use time sequencers: *First, next, then, after that, and now, finally.*

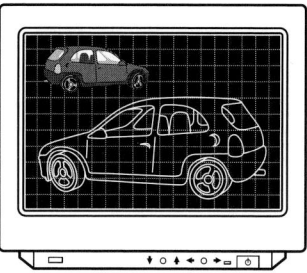

*First, the car **is designed** on computer with a CAD program. Next, ...*

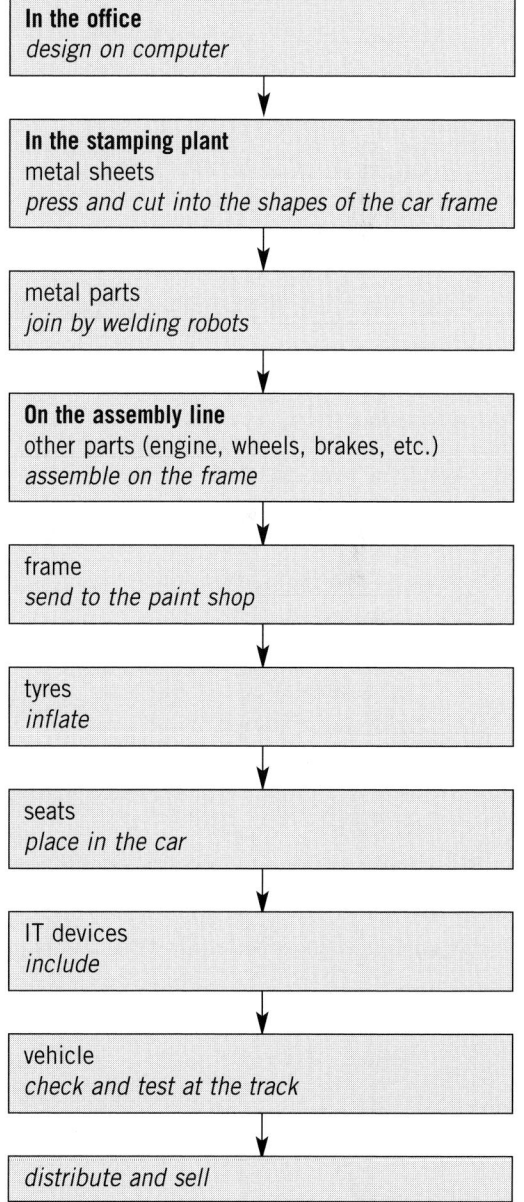

In the office
design on computer

↓

In the stamping plant
metal sheets
press and cut into the shapes of the car frame

↓

metal parts
join by welding robots

↓

On the assembly line
other parts (engine, wheels, brakes, etc.)
assemble on the frame

↓

frame
send to the paint shop

↓

tyres
inflate

↓

seats
place in the car

↓

IT devices
include

↓

vehicle
check and test at the track

↓

distribute and sell

Unit 25 *The Java revolution*

Vocabulary review: Java

1 Match these words with the correct explanation below.

1 applet
2 plug-in
3 file transfer
4 object-oriented
5 Java virtual machine
6 computer bug

a to copy a file from the Net to your PC
b an error in a program
c a programming environment that interprets Java for operating systems like Mac OS, UNIX or Windows
d a technique that allows the creation of 'objects' to represent processes in programming
e a small program produced with Java
f a program that adds capabilities to your browser (e.g. to play sound or video clips)

Reading: Landmarks in computer history

2 Read the text and find:

1 the device used in China 4,000 years ago
2 the first woman computer programmer
3 the distinction between first and second generation computers
4 the company that designed the first microprocessor
5 the OS designed for IBM PCs and compatibles
6 the first computer which used a graphical interface
7 the year when the Web was created
8 the company that invented Java

3 Translate these words into your language.

1 abacus
2 punched card
3 vacuum tube
4 transistor
5 silicon chip
6 compiler
7 cyberspace
8 optics
9 artificial intelligence
10 molecular computer

Landmarks in computer history

2000 BC The abacus emerged in Asia. It allowed people to make calculations using moving beads arranged on a rack.

1642 AD Blaise Pascal invented the first mechanical adding machine, a numerical wheel called Pascaline.

1833 Charles Babbage started to build his Analytical Engine, the forerunner of the modern computer. He was helped by Augusta Ada, who is considered the first female computer programmer.

1890 Herman Hollerith used punched cards in a device which automatically read the US census.

1941 Konrad Zuse built the first programmable computer, called Z3, working on the binary system.

First generation computers (1945–1954)

1945 The University of Pennsylvania designed ENIAC, an electronic computer which used vacuum tubes and was able to calculate at electronic speeds.

Second generation computers (1955–1964)
Computers used transistors instead of vacuum tubes. Memories were made of magnetizable cores (e.g. the IBM 1401).

Third generation computers (1965–1973)

1965 The first computers built using silicon chips went on sale (e.g. the IBM 360 and CDC 6400).

1971 Intel released the first microprocessor.

Fourth generation computers (1974–Present)
Computers became smaller as more components were squeezed onto microchips.

1975 MITS sold the first minicomputer, the Altair 8800. Bill Gates and Paul Allen founded Microsoft and wrote a BASIC compiler for the Altair.

1976 Steve Jobs and Steve Wozniak founded Apple Computer, Inc.

1981 IBM sold the IBM PC, a model that became the standard in personal computers. MS-DOS was the operating system for IBM PCs and compatibles.

1984 Apple produced the Macintosh, the first computer with a mouse and a graphical user interface (GUI).

1986 William Gibson invented the term 'cyberspace' in his novel *Neuromancer*.
1991 CERN (Conseil Européen pour la Recherche Nucléaire) created the World Wide Web.
1995 Microsoft launched Windows 95 and Sun Microsystems created the Java language.
2001 Intel launched the Pentium 4 running at 2 GHz.

Fifth generation computers (Present and beyond)
- Fibre optics and optical disks revolutionize the world of computers.
- Artificial Intelligence and voice recognition are incorporated into computer applications.
- Experts start making tiny, superfast computers known as nanocomputers. Some are electronic, others are biochemical (e.g. DNA computers) working with bio-chips made of millions of molecules.

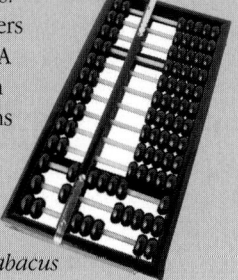

An abacus

4   **Look at the text again and put the verbs into the correct column.**

Regular past tenses in -ed	Irregular past tenses
....	....
....	....

Language work: Past tenses

5   **Look at the list and write sentences describing what Kelly did or didn't do last week.**

e.g. *Last Monday she began a course on Java.*

Monday	begin a course on Java (✓)
	phone parents (✗)
Tuesday	write an e-mail to a webpal (✓)
	watch TV (✗)
Wednesday	repair the optical drive (✗)
	visit her friend in hospital (✓)
Thursday	read the *Financial Times* (✗)
	send a postcard to a friend (✓)
Friday	have lunch with her boss (✓)
	go to her German class (✗)
Saturday	buy a DVD-R drive for brother (✓)
Sunday	download music from the Net (✓)

6   **Look at the sentences below. What is the verb tense called in each one?**

When the manager left the office ...

1   Yoshiko was using a mobile phone.
2   Tina was writing letters.
3   Hamid and Beata were talking about a project.
4   Franco and Anna were exploring the Web.

Writing: What were you doing?

7   **a   Study this dialogue. Identify the use of the past simple and past progressive.**

A: I broke my sister's pocket PC yesterday.
B: Really? What were you doing?
A: I was sitting on it.
B: And what did you do about it?
A: I told her. She was furious with me.

b   Write similar dialogues for these situations.

1   I realized I had a computer virus on my PC.
2   Someone stole my wallet.
3   My grandfather saw a UFO.

Past simple

I/you/he/she/we/they work**ed**.
I/you/he/she/we/they **didn't work**.
Did I/you/he/she/we/they **work**?

Irregular verbs: see list on page 78.

We use the past simple to talk about:
- a complete action or event which happened at a specific time in the past.

past   *I sent you an e-mail last week.*   now

Past progressive
was/were + -*ing* form
We use the past progressive to talk about:
- an action which was in progress at a definite time.

past   *I was chatting with some webpals.*   now
At one o'clock

- two or more actions happening at the same time.
  We were talking while she was reading the paper.
- We sometimes use the past **progressive** to describe the situation or 'background' action, and the past **simple** to describe the main action.
  *I **was playing** football when I **broke** my leg.*

Reading: Job advertisements

1 Look at these job advertisements. Write three important requirements for each job.

Webmaster

We are seeking a Webmaster for **eJupiter.com**, a company dedicated to e-commerce.
The successful candidate will manage our website. You will be responsible for making sure the web server runs properly. You will monitor the traffic through the site, and design and update our web pages.
Experience using HTML and Java; Adobe PDF and Photoshop (an advantage).
Knowledge of web editors: MS FrontPage or equivalent.

For further information, visit our website.

....
....
....

COMPUTER SALES ASSISTANT

This is a good opportunity to work for **PC Market**, the largest computer shop in the city. You must have some knowledge of operating systems and peripherals.
You will help the sales manager to install all kinds of software and sell computer products. Some experience in customer relations may be useful. Driving licence essential.

Send your CV to *PC Market*,
27 Castle Street, Cardiff SE2 3BA
phone: 01362 698385
e-mail: barnett@pcmarket.co.uk

....
....
....

2 Read this letter of application.

a Which job does it refer to?

b Put the verbs in brackets into the past simple or present perfect.

5 Cley Street
Swaffham
Norfolk NR8 3AT

3rd April

Personnel Manager
18, Oak Street
Norwich
Norfolk NR9 5QP

Dear Sir/Madam,
I am writing to apply for the post of .... which was advertised in the Evening News on April 3rd.
   After I left university in 1990 in France, I (1) (complete) .... a course on computer hardware and networking. Five years ago I (2) (do) .... a course on Web design at the Cybernetics College. Here I (3) (learn) .... how to use HTML and the Java language.
   I (4) (study) .... languages at school and, when I was a teenager, I (5) (spend) .... six months in Morocco; I am fluent in French, English and Arabic.
   For the last three years I (6) (work) .... part-time in Keo.com, where I (7) (be) .... responsible for updating their website regularly.
   Since May this year I (8) (use) .... Macromedia Flash to create media animation. I really enjoy working on the Web.
   I enclose a curriculum vitae and samples of my work. I will be available for an interview at any time.
   I look forward to hearing from you.

   Yours faithfully,
   Françoise Corrigan

Language work: Present perfect

3 Look at the box opposite. Put these verbs into the present perfect or past simple tense.

1 I (just send) .... a letter of application.

2 (you ever work) .... as a web designer?

3 A: Have you seen that film before?
   B: Yes, I (see) .... it when I was a child.

4 It was still raining when I (finish) .... work.

5 I sent you the artwork brief last Saturday. (you receive) .... it yet?

6 They (get married) ……………….............
  two years ago.

7 She (be) ……………… a software engineer
  since 2001.

4 Complete the sentences with *for*, *since*, *ago*, *already* or *yet*.

1 Have you repaired the hard disk
  ………………?

2 No, I haven't repaired it ………………

3 Yes, I have ……………… repaired it.

4 She has been a graphics designer
  ……………… about five years.

5 I finished my science degree five months
  ………………

6 I've been studying English ……………… I
  was ten.

Present perfect simple
Have/has + past participle

We use this tense to talk about:
• completed actions connected to the present.
  *I **have repaired** the computer. (= it works now)*
• personal experiences
  *I **have never been** to Paris.*
• past actions in a time up to now where we put emphasis on the quantity or number (how many?)
  *She **has failed** three subjects.*
• states that started in the past and continue to the present
  *I've **been** a software developer since 1994.*
  'Since' refers to a point in time.
  *I've **been** a software developer for 10 years.*
  'For' refers to a period of time.

Present perfect progressive
Have/has been + present participle

We use this tense to talk about:
• actions which started in the past and are still happening
  I've been painting my room for two hours.
• past actions or situations in progress, with emphasis on duration (how long?)
  She's been sending faxes all morning.

---

5 Put the verbs into the present perfect simple or the present perfect progressive.

1 Jan (complain) ……………… all morning.

2 They (work) ……………… on the project all day.

3 Jeff (just pass) ……………… his driving test.

4 How many letters (you write) ………………
  today?

5 They (interview) ……………… six candidates
  today.

6 She (write) ……………… this essay since
  9 o'clock.

7 (you wait) ……………… for a long time?

Writing: Applying for a job

6 Angela Russell is interested in the job of *Computer sales assistant* (exercise 1). Use her CV to write a letter applying for the job. Follow these steps:

Greeting: Dear Sir / Madam,

Paragraph 1: reason for writing

Paragraph 2: education and qualifications

Paragraph 3: work experience / present job

Paragraph 4: Other details (e.g. interests)

Paragraph 5: availability for interview

Closing: Yours faithfully,

You can start like this:
I am writing to apply for the post of …

Notes for Curriculum Vitae

Education:
• three A levels and one year diploma in IT
Qualifications:
• Knowledge of Windows, Mac OS and Linux
• Familiar with a wide range of programs,
  e.g. MS Office
Work experience:
• Employed two years as a data entry operator
• Experience in installing and testing PCs and
  peripherals
Other details:
• Hobbies: Net surfing, music, travelling
• Driving licence and car
• Good communicator with clients

Unit 27 *Electronic communications*

Vocabulary review: Abbreviations

1 **What's the meaning of these abbreviations?**

> modem   kbps   ISP   ADSL   BBS   FTP   IRC

Reading: An instant message

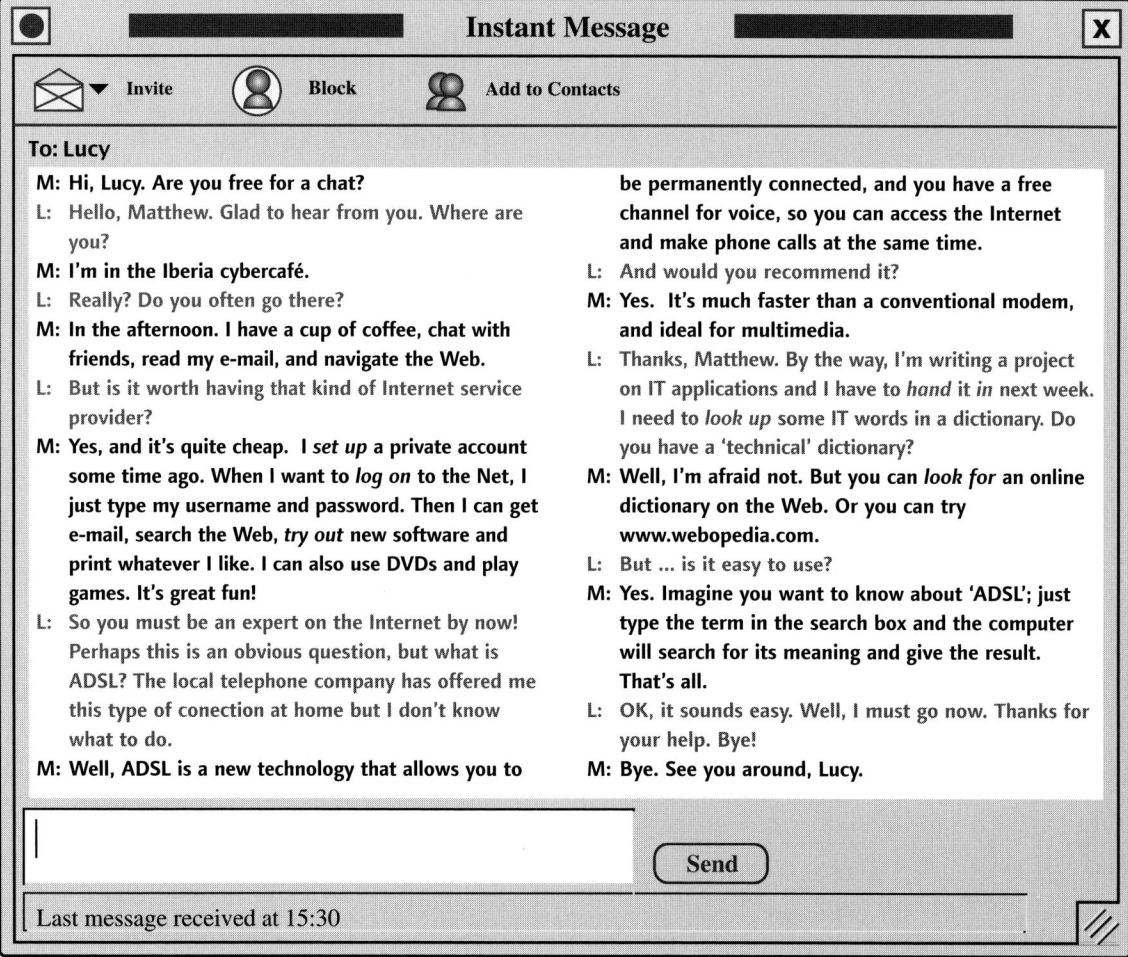

Instant Message   X

▼ Invite   Block   Add to Contacts

To: Lucy

M: Hi, Lucy. Are you free for a chat?

L: Hello, Matthew. Glad to hear from you. Where are you?

M: I'm in the Iberia cybercafé.

L: Really? Do you often go there?

M: In the afternoon. I have a cup of coffee, chat with friends, read my e-mail, and navigate the Web.

L: But is it worth having that kind of Internet service provider?

M: Yes, and it's quite cheap. I *set up* a private account some time ago. When I want to *log on* to the Net, I just type my username and password. Then I can get e-mail, search the Web, *try out* new software and print whatever I like. I can also use DVDs and play games. It's great fun!

L: So you must be an expert on the Internet by now! Perhaps this is an obvious question, but what is ADSL? The local telephone company has offered me this type of conection at home but I don't know what to do.

M: Well, ADSL is a new technology that allows you to be permanently connected, and you have a free channel for voice, so you can access the Internet and make phone calls at the same time.

L: And would you recommend it?

M: Yes. It's much faster than a conventional modem, and ideal for multimedia.

L: Thanks, Matthew. By the way, I'm writing a project on IT applications and I have to *hand* it *in* next week. I need to *look up* some IT words in a dictionary. Do you have a 'technical' dictionary?

M: Well, I'm afraid not. But you can *look for* an online dictionary on the Web. Or you can try www.webopedia.com.

L: But ... is it easy to use?

M: Yes. Imagine you want to know about 'ADSL'; just type the term in the search box and the computer will search for its meaning and give the result. That's all.

L: OK, it sounds easy. Well, I must go now. Thanks for your help. Bye!

M: Bye. See you around, Lucy.

Send

Last message received at 15:30

2 **Read the instant message and find answers to these questions.**

1 What does Matthew do to log on to the Internet?

2 What services are offered by the cybercafé?

3 What are the advantages of having an ADSL connection?

4 Why does Lucy need a technical dictionary?

5 Which dictionary does Matthew recommend to her?

3 **Here are some verbs from the text. Match them with their definitions on the right.**

1 set up   a find out by looking in a
2 log on   reference book or dictionary
3 try out   b establish, create
4 hand in   c search, try to find
5 look up   d start using a system by entering
6 look for   a name and a password
                    e deliver, present
                    f test it in order to find how
                       effective or useful it is

58

Language work: Verbs with particles

4 Match the verbs on the left with their equivalent on the right. Use a dictionary if necessary.

1	run out	a	keep copies of
2	carry out	b	be finished, used completely
3	back up	c	occupy
4	give away	d	distribute freely
5	sort out	e	form the parts of
6	make up	f	connect
7	take up	g	arrange, classify
8	plug into	h	execute, fulfil

5 Now use the correct form of verbs in exercise 4 to complete the following sentences.

1 The CPU .... program instructions.
2 Most printers use ink cartridges or toner which can be replaced when they ....
3 In a database, a special function can .... data into different order, such as alphabetical order.
4 When a PC fails, you can lose your data. This is why you need to .... all your important files.
5 Music .... a lot of space on disk.
6 Some computer magazines .... a CD-ROM full of public domain software.
7 Games consoles are games machines which you .... a TV set.
8 Thousands of networks .... the Internet.

6 Match the responses in a–f to sentences 1–6.

1 Do you take part in 'newsgroups' on the Net?
2 What happens to the data in the RAM section when the computer is **switched off**?
3 How can I get a free copy of this software?
4 I want to end the session. Shall I **log off**?
5 When do you want me to **bring back** those CDs?
6 Why was the hacker arrested?

a The data is lost.
b Just **fill in** this form with your name and address, and send it to Microsoft.

c Yes, but don't shut the computer down; I want to print out a report.
d Yes, I use them to **find out** more about my interests.
e Because he **broke into** a computer system and stole confidential data.
f Oh, whenever you've finished with them.

Verbs with particles

Most of them have an idiomatic meaning (which is not predictable from the meaning of the parts).
e.g. He **gave up** smoking. = He stopped smoking.

There are two main categories:
a In **phrasal verbs**, the particle is an adverb, e.g. *The plane took off.*
   Many phrasal verbs take a direct object.
   Please <u>turn on</u> the computer.   (= connect)
   I've <u>handed in</u> my resignation.   (= present)
b A **prepositional verb** consists of a lexical verb followed by a preposition associated with it.
   We must <u>go into</u> the cost.   (= examine)
   He's <u>looking after</u> the child.   (= take care)

Distinction

Compare the phrasal verb LOOK UP ('find') and the prepositional verb LOOK FOR ('search').
a The particle of a phrasal verb precedes or follows the direct object, but the particle of a prepositional verb must precede the object.
   a *I need to look **up** this word.* ✓
   b *I need to look this word **up**.* ✓
   c *I'm looking **for** a dictionary.* ✓
   d *I'm looking a dictionary **for**.* not correct
b When the object is a personal pronoun, the pronoun precedes the particle of a phrasal verb, but follows the particle of a prepositional verb.
   a *I need to look **it** up.*   ✓
   b *I need to look up **it**.*   not correct
   c *I'm looking **it** for.*   not correct
   d *I'm looking for **it**.*   ✓

Verbs with two particles

Some verbs combine adverb + preposition.
I'm <u>looking forward to</u> my holidays. (= anticipate with pleasure)
I can't <u>put up with</u> his behaviour. (= tolerate)

Unit 28 *Internet issues*

Vocabulary review: Security

1 Solve the clues and complete the puzzle.

1 An e-mail address consists of a u.............. (or nickname) followed by an @.

2 A private network within a single organization is often called i.............

3 Internet s.............. is crucial when sending credit card numbers or confidential information.

4 Internet Explorer allows you to disable or delete c.............. – small files stored on your hard disk by web servers to know when you visited their site.

5 Structured Query Language is used for requesting information from a database.

6 It's well known that v.............. can enter a PC through files from disks or from the Net.

7 An intranet (company network) is protected from unauthorized users by a special program called a 'f..............'.

8 An Internet f.............. is a type of program that lets parents restrict access to specific aspects of the Web.

9 There are e.............. systems that encode information so that unauthorized users can't read it.

10 An 18-year-old h.............. has been arrested in connection with virus propagation.

Down This term refers to the rules of etiquette or 'good manners' when using the Internet.

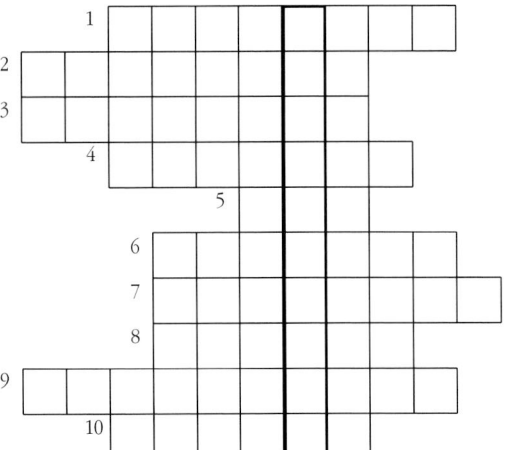

Reading: Internet history

2 Read the text to find out how the Internet has evolved. Write down the facts corresponding to these dates.

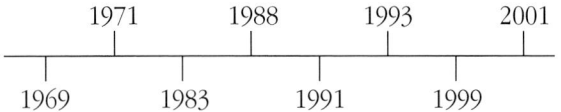

1971   1988   1993   2001

1969   1983   1991   1999

3 Look at the text again. Put the verbs into the past.

e.g. *The US Defence Advanced Research Projects Agency **established** …*

> ### *Internet history*
>
> 1969 The US Defence Advanced Research Projects Agency establishes ARPANET, a wide area network connecting research centres.
> 1971 Ray Tomlinson of BBN invents an e-mail program to send messages across a network. The @ sign is chosen for its 'at' meaning.
> 1973 ARPANET makes first international connections.
> 1974 V. Cerf and B. Kahn publish 'A Protocol for Packet Network Interconnection'.
> 1979 A collection of forums (newsgroups) constitute USENET.
> 1981 BITNET, short for 'Because It's Time NETwork', provides e-mail and file transfers to universities.
> 1982 TCP-IP is adopted as the standard language of the Internet.
> 1983 The most important networks (ARPANET, MILnet and CSnet) are interconnected.
> 1985 The Domain Name System is created.
> 1988 Jarkko Oikarinen develops the system known as Internet Relay Chat.
> 1991 CERN (Conseil Européen pour la Recherche Nucléaire) develops the World Wide Web. Philip Zimmerman writes *Pretty Good Privacy*, a program which protects e-mail messages.
> 1993 Marc Andreesen and the University of Illinois develop *Mosaic*, the first program that allows users to surf the Web.
> 1995 Commercial online systems (Compuserve, AOL, etc.) start providing Internet access. RealNetworks creates the RealAudio plug-in, which lets you hear audio files in real-time.

▶

1996 Netscape (*Navigator*) and Microsoft (*Internet Explorer*) start a battle to get people to use their Web browser. Java and Internet phone are the best technologies of the year.

1998 The Internet 2 network is born. This can handle huge packets of data and video at high speed.

1999 Online banking, e-commerce and MP3 music become fashionable.

2001 Napster lets users download MP3 music files. But a federal judge rules that Napster's technology is an infringement on the copyright of music.

Language work: Past perfect

4 Join the beginnings and endings to make sensible sentences.

Beginnings

1 They got married
2 After we'd finished work
3 Linda was very depressed
4 When she had typed all the letters

Endings

a because she had lost her job.
b we went for a walk.
c she decided to have a rest.
d just a week after they had fallen in love.

5 Write what each person had been doing. Choose verbs from the list.

e.g. *She felt exhausted. She had been working all day.*

design work hack smoke wait use

1 They .... for hours by the time I got home.
2 How long (you) .... in the company before it closed?
3 Before the website went live, he .... pages for months.
4 She .... into bank networks for 10 years before she was arrested.
5 Tony's eyes felt really sore and tired. He .... the computer for five hours.
6 When Rohan went into his office he could smell smoke. Someone .... in there.

6 Look at the picture. When the staff arrived this morning, they found that robbers had broken into the bank.

What had they done? Write five sentences using the past perfect. e.g. *They had broken ...*

> **Useful nouns**
> *window, security alarm, video camera, computer, bank account, data, bank notes, coins, money*
> **Useful verbs**
> *break, disconnect, switch on, steal, drop, paint, rob, take*

Past perfect simple

We form this tense with **had + past participle**:
She had written a letter.
We use this tense to talk about:
• an action which happened before another past action.
  *He **felt** satisfied because he **had found** a new job.*

past	new job	felt	now
	past perfect	past simple	▲

Past perfect progressive

We form this tense with **had been + present participle**:
She had been writing e-mails.

We use this tense to talk about:
• an action continuing up to a specific time in the past.
  *The criminals **had been stealing** information for years before the police caught them.*
• a continuous past action which had a visible effect. We put the emphasis on 'how long'.
  *My eyes were irritated because **I'd been crying** all morning.*

Vocabulary review: Networks

1 **Network quiz**

Choose the answers.

1 This type of network links computers in a small area, such as a single room or building.
a LAN b WAN c Intranet

2 A computer that holds data and programs for other computers on a network is called
a webmaster b hub c file server

3 Any hardware device connected to a local area network is called
a a token b a node c Ethernet

4 On networks, this set of rules is used to determine the formats by which data may be exchanged between different computer systems.
a router b architecture c protocol

5 ADSL is a high-speed Internet connection over the telephone lines.
a True b False

6 Which network cables are faster?
a telephone wires b coaxial cables c fibre-optic cables

7 TCP/IP is the language computers use to communicate with each other on the Internet.
a True b False

Language work: Prepositions of place

2 **Choose the correct preposition.**

inside		between		on	in
by	at		into		out of

1 Networks are interconnected .... devices called 'gateways'.
2 Fibre-optic cables transmit data .... high speed.
3 The hard disk drive is .... a sealed case.
4 Data flows .... the processor and the main memory.
5 The modem is .... my desk.
6 Maria is .... her office. She's typing at the computer.
7 She walked .... the conference in protest.
8 They got .... the car and drove off.

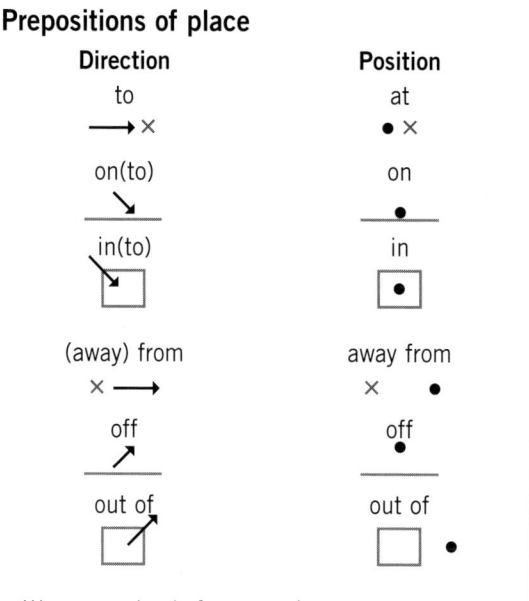

Prepositions of place

Direction	Position
to	at
on(to)	on
in(to)	in
(away) from	away from
off	off
out of	out of

- We use *arrive in* for countries or towns and *arrive at* for specific places.
  *She arrived **in** London / **at** the airport at 10.*

Prepositions indicating relative position

- opposite *The bank is **opposite** my school.*
  *= My school is **opposite** the bank.*
- above / below
  A   *A is **above** the line.*
  B   *B is **below** the line.*
- in front of / behind
  Katie ↔ Sue ↔ Tom
  *Katie is **in front of** Sue in class. Tom is **behind** Sue.*
- **Above** and **below** are similar to **over** and **under** respectively, though the latter tend to mean 'directly above' and 'directly below'.
  ***over** the bridge / **under** a tree*
- by / next to / beside
  *She left the keys **by** / **next to** / **beside** her laptop.*
- Compare **between** with **among**.
  *John is sitting **between** Mary and Sara.*

  ● John ●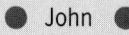

  *There was a house **among** the trees.*
  *= There were trees **round** the house.*

Writing: Describing an office

3 Describe the furniture and computer equipment in this office.
Use prepositions of position.

4 **Read the box. Write questions as in the example.**

e.g. *I went to Italy with my sister.*
   = **Who** *did you go* **with**?

1 She is talking <u>about ARPANET</u>, the
   precursor of the Internet.
   ....

2 Gianni is going out <u>with a computer expert</u>.
   ....

3 I sent the fax <u>to the Systems Analyst</u>.
   ....

4 My brother works <u>for IBM</u>.
   ....

5 **Change the sentences as in the example.**

e.g. *It's a pleasure to work with her.*
   = *She is a pleasure to work with.*

1 It's difficult to get to the city centre.
   ....

2 It's nice to talk to him.
   ....

3 It's uncomfortable to travel in small cars.
   ....

4 It's boring to play chess with Dina.
   ....

Prepositions at the end of sentences

In some circumstances prepositions go at the end:
a when the interrogative pronoun has a
   preposition as its complement:
   *What are you looking **at**?*
b when the subject of a passive sentence
   corresponds to the complement in the active voice:
   We have paid for the connection.
   = *The connection has been paid **for**.*
c after infinitives in structures like:
   *She is a pleasure to talk **to**.*

Unit 30 *New technologies*

Language work: Future forms

1 **Revise the future forms in the box. Then choose the correct answer.**

1 I promise
   a I'll buy you a 3G mobile phone.
   b I'm going to buy you a 3G mobile phone.
   c I'm buying you a 3G mobile phone.

2 A: Would you like to come to my party tomorrow?
   B: I'm afraid I can't.
   a I'll meet Bob at the airport.
   b I'm meeting Bob at the airport.
   c I meet Bob at the airport.

3 In the near future, PCs
   a communicate with other devices without cables.
   b are going to communicate with other devices without cables.
   c will communicate with other devices without cables.

4 Please call me as soon as
   a you finish the project.
   b you will finish the project.
   c you will have finished the project.

5 A: My laptop has crashed!
   B: Don't worry.
   a I'm lending you mine.
   b I'll lend you mine.
   c I'm going to lend you mine.

2 **What is going to happen? Look at the pictures and write predictions as in the example.**

They are going to have dinner.

1
....
....
....
....

2
....
....
....
....

3
....
....
....
....

4
....
....
....
....

5
....
....
....
....

3 Complete this conversation using either the present progressive or *will + verb*.

JORGE: I hear you're going on holiday next week.

CARMEN: Yes, we (1) (go) .... to Paris. I can't wait.

JORGE: I think you (2) (love) .... Paris. How (3) (you travel) .... ?

CARMEN: Well, first we (4) (fly) .... from Madrid and we (5) (stay) .... in Paris for five days.

JORGE: That sounds great! Are you going to any theme parks near Paris?

CARMEN: Yes, actually, we (6) (visit) .... EuroDisney. After that, we're going to the south of France. We probably (7) (stop) .... at Futuroscope, near Poitiers. It's a theme park based on new technologies, virtual reality, 3-D images, ...

JORGE: How lovely! When are you coming back home?

CARMEN: Well, I don't know. I have a month's holiday, so I hope we just (8) (relax) .... by the sea for a few days and then ...

Writing: Making predictions

4 Write your own predictions about these topics.

1 Space tourism
e.g. *In the year 2010 there will be sightseeing trips to the moon.*
Yours: ....
....

2 The Internet
e.g. *Everyone will have high speed access to the Internet.*
Yours: ....
....

3 Mobile phones
e.g. *They will be able to send MMS (Multimedia short messages).*
Yours: ....
....

4 Health and genetics
e.g. *Electronic chips will be implanted inside our body to detect possible illnesses.*
Yours: ....
....

5 Intelligent homes
e.g. *Robots will do the housework for us.*
Yours: ....
....

5 Look at the box. Translate these sentences into your language.

1 Please don't call tonight. I'll be taking part in a videoconference.

2 He says he won't have finished the report by Monday.

3 The technician will have repaired the computer by Friday.

4 Some day, we'll be talking to our PC naturally, like a friend.

5 Next June she'll have been teaching for 30 years.

6 In a few years' time students will be using handheld and wearable computers in class.

Other future forms

Future progressive (*will be* + present participle)
To talk about actions in progress at a stated future time.
This time next Saturday I'll be skiing.

Future perfect simple (*will have* + past participle)
To talk about actions finished at a stated future time.
By the end of June I will have finished my exams.

Future perfect progressive
To emphasize 'how long'.
By February I will have been working here for three years.

Answer key

Unit 1: *Computer applications*

1

1 d 2 c 3 a 4 b 5 c 6 a 7 b

2 *Possible questions and answers*
1 Does Gina listen to MP3 music?
  Yes, she does.
2 Does Gina write e-mails?
  No, she doesn't.
3 Do Paul and Sue read magazines?
  No, they don't.
4 Do Paul and Sue play computer games?
  Yes, they do.
5 Do Paul and Sue write e-mails?
  Yes, they do.
6 Do you read magazines / listen to MP3 music?
  Yes, I do. / No, I don't.
7 Do you play computer games / write e-mails?
  Yes, I do. / No, I don't.

3
1 What do you do in the evenings?
2 Do you search for information on the Net?
3 What type of films do you like?
4 How many foreign languages do you speak?
5 Do you chat with strangers on the Web?

4

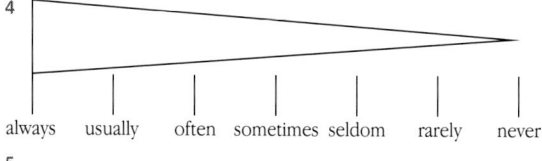

always   usually   often   sometimes   seldom   rarely   never

5
1 I often receive SMS messages on my mobile phone.
2 Jan sometimes sends articles to newsgroups.
3 Do you usually help your friends with their homework?
4 He is always complaining.
5 They have never seen a UFO.

6 *Possible answers*
1 She writes e-mails every day.
2 She watches TV in the evening.
3 She goes to college on weekdays.
4 She plays basketball on Saturdays.
5 She travels abroad three times a year.
6 She goes to the cinema twice a week.
7 She goes to a local pub once a week.

7 *Possible answer*
• Industrial robots are used:
  to weld cars
  to make and package products
  to build machines
• Micro-machines and insect-sized robots are used:
  to monitor the heart rate and blood pressure;
  to help doctors in heart operations and surgery.
• Robots are used in dangerous situations:
  to repair nuclear plants, clean toxic wastes, defuse bombs

• Gadgets are used to control activities in 'intelligent homes'.
• Androids will be used to access the Internet, guide the blind, assist elderly people, act as security guards.

8
1 Artificial Intelligence   2 software
3 assembly line   4 gadgets   5 androids

Unit 2: *Computer essentials*

1

```
D  R  I  V  E     R  A  M        H
                                 A
         S  C  A  N  N  E  R      R  M
                                 D  O
      M                          W  D
P  R  O  C  E  S  S  O  R         A  E
R     U                          R  M
I     S  D     R  O  M            E
N     E  I
T        S     M  O  N  I  T  O  R
E        K
R           S  O  F  T  W  A  R  E
```

2
There are three basic types of portable computers ... consisting of ... Others include ...

3

From general to specific	From specific to general
1 There are two classes of personal computers	4 The ... make up the CPU ...
	5 The ... constitute ...
2 ... consists of two parts ...	6 A DVD is a type of disk.
3 ... is made up ...	7 A hub is a component of ...

4 *Open task*

5
1 digital   2 computer   3 chip   4 sends
5 data   6 Internet   7 cables

Unit 3: *Inside the system*

1
CPU   Central Processing Unit
ALU   Arithmetic Logic Unit
GHz   Gigahertz
RAM   Random Access Memory
ROM   Read Only Memory
DIMM   Dual In-Line Memory Module

2
a cyber-thriller which captures the audience's attention ...
a storyline that combines action, science fiction ...
a virtual environment ..., where (relative adverb) people are just slaves ...
AI machines which generate energy from human bodies.
a computer hacker that looks for an answer to ...
'agents', who are really machines in human form.
a reality beyond reality that controls human lives.
the character who tries to kill Neo.
'The One' who will liberate humankind ...

66

3

We use **who** for people and **which** for things.
We can use **that** for both people and things.

4

1 whose   2 which   3 where   4 who   5 that

5

2 A CD-ROM drive is a common storage device which/that reads data from a CD-ROM disk.
3 An anti-virus program is a type of software which/that protects your computer from viruses.
4 A hacker is a person who/that invades a network's privacy.
5 A palmtop is a very small computer which/that can be held in one hand.
6 A software engineer is a person who writes software.

6

1 Have you got a video camera I can use?
3 That is the girl I met at the conference.
5 That's the film I was talking about.
6 Have you read the report Jack wrote last week?

7

1 It was Mary who broke your camera.
2 It was a spaceship that I saw, not a UFO.
3 It was last Friday that I bought a DVD.

8

1 RAM   2 secondary storage (disks)   3 RAM
4 ROM   5 RAM   6 ROM   7 secondary storage (disks)

Unit 4: *Bits and bytes*

1

1 bit   2 byte   3 kilobyte   4 megabyte
5 gigabyte   6 terabyte

2

1 b byte
2 d and f MB
3 a 3 kilobytes
4 c RAM
5 g 56 kilobits per second
6 e 17 gigabytes
7 f Because there is not enough space on disk

3

Number: gigahertz
Time and order: pre-recorded
Location: intercity
Attitude: cooperating
Size or degree: macroeconomics
Negative: unlucky

4

1 e   2 b   3 f   4 g   5 a   6 d   7 c

5

1 reboot   2 anti-glare   3 subtitles
4 interconnected   5 teletext   6 cooperation

6

Size or degree

super-   supermarket, superman
hyper-   hypertext, hypersensitive
mini-   minidisk, mini-skirt
micro-   microchip, microprocessor
semi-   semi-circle, semi-final
ultra-   ultra-violet, ultra-light

Number

uni-   uniform, unisex
mono-   monologue, monosyllable
bi-   binary, bicycle
multi-   multi-racial, multimedia
kilo-   kilogram(me), kilowatt
mega-   megabyte, megahertz
giga-   gigabyte, gigahertz

7

1 invisible   2 disagree   3 unable
4 misleading   5 illogical

8

1 unaware   2 illegitimate   3 impatient   4 irrational
5 imperfect   6 unexpected   7 impartial   8 impractical
9 dishonest   10 unclean

Unit 5: *Buying a computer*

1

1 d   2 c   3 b   4 e   5 e   6 g   7 a   8 f

2

1 performance   2 notebook   3 drive   4 CD   5 display
6 anti-virus   7 keyboard   8 microphone   9 peripherals

3

> Microprocessor: 3 GHz
> RAM: 512 MB
> Hard disk: 60 GB
> Screen: 14.1" TFT active matrix, 16 m. colours, 1024 x 768 pixel resolution
> Operating system: Windows XP
> Other software: Lotus SmartSuite, Adobe Acrobat Reader, Internet Explorer and anti-virus
> Other peripherals: keyboard, touch pad, SoundBlaster card, stereo speakers, microphone, 56k modem
> Power supply: rechargeable Lithium batteries

4

2 She is using a mobile phone.   3 They are buying a computer.
4 She is eating a sandwich.   5 He is reading a book.
6 She is swimming.

5

2 He isn't showing some customers round the company on Tuesday. He's flying to Los Angeles.
3 He isn't having lunch with the production manager on Wednesday. He's having lunch with the sales manager.
4 He isn't having a business meeting on Thursday. He is doing a radio interview about the effect of technology on the environment.
6 He isn't going to the theatre on Saturday evening. He's going to the movies.
7 His girlfriend isn't coming to see him on Sunday afternoon. He's watching a football match.

6

1 I am thinking about his plan.
2 Do you have a webcam?
3 I don't know where she lives.
4 This perfume smells of lemons.
5 Mary is seeing her boyfriend.
6 I hear you are going on holiday soon.
7 Are you enjoying this game?

Unit 6: *Type, click and talk!*

1

1 d 2 j 3 e 4 l 5 b 6 f 7 k 8 a 9 h

2 *Possible answers*

A printer is an output device which prints out text or graphics on paper.
A digital camera is used to store images as digital (binary) data, which can then be processed by a PC.
A touch screen is a touch-sensitive display which lets you use your finger to point directly to objects on the screen.
A microphone is an input device which allows you to record your own sounds and to interact with your PC by voice.

3

1 A barcode reader is an input device that scans the barcodes on products.
2 Barcodes are made of modules that identify the general category of the product, the manufacturer, the brand name, the price, etc.
3 Barcode readers are used to check the prices of the products at the supermarket. The data is also recorded on disk, so computers can keep a record of what articles are in stock and can instantly give orders for new supplies.
4 A computer system reads the details from a magnetic strip on the credit card and checks the data with the bank.
5 A smart card

4

1 c 2 d 3 a 4 e 5 b

5 *Possible answers*

In bookshops, barcode scanners can help the shop assistant to check the price of books and magazines, and to control the goods that are in stock. The data may be entered directly into a central processor or recorded on disk for future use. Barcodes can also contain secret information for security purposes.
In pharmacies, barcode scanners can automatically scan data from medicines and control the medicines available. The central computer can then keep a record of what items are in stock.

Unit 7: *Capture your favourite image*

1

1 long	longer	the longest
2 boring	more boring	the most boring
3 wet	wetter	the wettest
4 good	better	the best
5 attractive	more attractive	the most attractive
6 pretty	prettier	the prettiest
7 modern	more modern	the most modern
8 exciting	more exciting	the most exciting

2 *Possible answers*

1 A desktop PC is bigger than a laptop.
  A laptop is less powerful than a desktop PC.
  A desktop PC is heavier than a laptop.
  A laptop is not as fast as a desktop PC.
2 Women are more intelligent than men.
  Men are less patient than women.
  Women are more sensible than men.
  Men are stronger than women.

3

1 most popular   2 largest   3 most influential
4 smallest   5 most powerful   6 worst

4 *Open task*

5

1 most fluently   2 earlier   3 harder   4 worse   5 later
6 fastest   7 more beautifully / the most beautifully
8 more neatly

6

Correct rules: 1, 3

7

1 She is not old enough to do everything she wants.
2 My Internet connection is too slow.
3 The laser printer was too expensive.

8 *Open task*

Unit 8: *Viewing the output*

1

		1	R	E	F	R	E	S	H	
2	R	E	S	O	L	U	T	I	O	N
		3	B	E	A	M				
	4	F	I	L	T	E	R			
					■					
		5	D	I	S	P	L	A	Y	
	6	F	L	I	C	K	E	R		
		7	C	A	R	D				
8	P	I	X	E	L	S				
		9	H	E	R	T	Z			
10	C	O	N	T	R	A	S	T		

2

1 True
2 False. Flat-panel screens require less space than CRT monitors.
3 False. Liquid-crystal displays are flat. (CRTs are curved.)
4 True
5 True
6 False. Flat screens are more expensive than CRT monitors.
7 False. A flat-screen monitor is easy to adjust for tilt and height.

3

Cathode Ray Tube (a picture tube used by PC monitors and TV sets)

Liquid-Crystal Display

Television

Personal Computer

Thin Film Transistor (a technology that allows for clear and stable images)

Universal Serial Bus (an interface that lets you plug-and-play a lot of peripherals easily)

4 *Possible answers*

DO

First, **decide** whether you need a desktop PC or a portable.

Try the computer system before you buy it.

Before buying peripherals, **read** a few brochures.

Choose a suitable monitor for your needs.

Check that all the components work properly.

If you don't know how to configure hardware and software, **look for** professional advice.

When in doubt, **read and follow** the instructions in a computer guide.

Make back-ups of important files.

Insert disks into disk drives carefully.

Keep CDs and DVDs away from humidity and high temperatures.

Open an Internet account with a reliable service provider.

Keep your network password secret.

Be cautious about sending confidential information via e-mail.

All these examples can be rewritten like this:

You **should / ought to** buy ...

DON'T

Don't buy a PC just to play games.

If you are a beginner, **don't try** to install the hardware (monitor, printer, modem, etc.) yourself.

Don't use commercial software without a licence.

Don't open e-mails from strangers.

Don't touch the screen.

Don't propagate viruses through the Net.

All these examples can be rewritten like this:

You **shouldn't / oughtn't** to buy ...

5

1 shouldn't / had better not

2 should / had better

3 shouldn't / had better not

4 should / had better

5 should / had better

6

1 and 3   2 and 4

7

1 needn't   2 mustn't   3 have to   4 has to

5 mustn't   6 needn't

Unit 9: *Choosing a printer*

1

1 HP printers understand the PCL language.

2 PostScript was created in 1982.

3 Scalable fonts can be enlarged or reduced.

4 The 'prolog' of a PostScript file contains the sub-routines used to form different graphic elements.

5 PostScript is understood by imagesetters.

6 PostScript supports audio and video formats.

2

1 b   2 d   3 c   4 e   5 a

3 *Possible answers*

1 *Repetitions*:

PDL, printers, language, font, graphics, prolog, script, sub-routine, output, devices, etc.

2 *Synonyms*:

shape = outline

page description language = printer language

developed = created

enlarge or reduce the character to any size = without distortions

3 *Collocations*:

laser printer

dot-matrix printer

ink-jet printer

scalable font

4 *Superordinates*:

printer languages

printers

geometrical objects

graphic elements

output devices

drawing programs

Hyponyms:

Examples of printers: dot-matrix, imagesetter, laser, LaserJet, ink-jet, DeskJet

Examples of geometrical objects: lines, arcs, circles

Examples of graphic elements: squares, curves

Examples of output devices: printer, imagesetter, film recorder

Examples of drawing programs: *Illustrator, Freehand, CorelDraw*

4

1 both of which refers to 'Adobe PostScript and Hewlett Packard PCL'.

2 their refers to 'Hewlett Packard'.

3 it refers to PostScript'.

4 This refers to 'vectorial format ... as geometric descriptions'.

5 which refers to 'script'.

6 that refers to 'hardware'.

7 such as qualifies 'Drawing programs' specified by the following words *Illustrator, Freehand* or *CorelDraw*.

5

Open task

Unit 10: *I/O devices for the disabled*

1

1 magnification software   2 word processor
3 screen reader   4 voice recognition
5 expansion slots   6 database   7 websites

2

1 a password   2 a swimming pool   3 a chequebook
4 a dining room   5 traffic lights   6 a phone card

3 *Possible answers*

1 a person who writes software
2 a device which reads and writes data on a disk
3 a computer which stores files for other computers in a network
4 a person who analyses systems
5 a device which inputs data into a computer
6 a type of printer which uses laser technology
7 a shop which sells books
NOTE: *who* and *which* can be replaced by *that*.

4

disk: hard disk, disk error, optical disk, floppy disk, disk drive, disk directory, compact disk
-ware: shareware, freeware, firmware, software, hardware
web: web mail, wordweb, webpal, website, web designer, webpage

Unit 11: *Magnetic drives*

1

1 floppy disk   2 hard drive   3 Zip drive   4 microdrive
5 Formatting   6 tracks, sectors   7 access time
8 defragmentation

2

1   *noun*   *adverb*   *adj*   *noun*
    provi<u>der</u>   usual<u>ly</u>   month<u>ly</u>   connec<u>tion</u>
2   *adj*   *adj*   *adj*   *adj*
    eras<u>able</u>   optic<u>al</u>   expens<u>ive</u>   magne<u>tic</u>
3   *adj*   *noun*   *noun*
    electron<u>ic</u>   entertain<u>ment</u> us<u>ers</u>
4   *noun*   *adj*   *noun*
    inform<u>ation</u>   virt<u>ual</u>   shopp<u>ing</u>

3

Nouns	Verbs	Adjectives	Adverbs
measurement	threaten	colourful	quickly
partnership	criticize	harmless	electronically
disinfectant	stimulate	affirmative	eastward
journalist	purify	dirty	clockwise

4

1 advertisement   6 resistance   11 transformation
2 programming   7 organization   12 development
3 employment   8 attachment   13 imagination
4 meeting   9 processing   14 insurance
5 performance   10 compilation

5

1 dangerous   5 successful   9 creative
2 helpful   6 personal   10 interactive
3 powerful   7 attractive   11 enjoyable
4 professional   8 negotiable   12 protective

6

1 computerize   2 computational   3 computer
4 browser   5 Browsing   6 browse

7

1 multimedia   2 gigabytes   3 drive   4 time   5 secure
6 protection   7 compatible   8 highest   9 visit

Unit 12: *Optical breakthrough*

1

1 What's a DVD?   2 DVDs versus CDs
3 DVD formats   4 Configurations of data layers
5 Looking forward

2

1 MPEG-2
  Note: This is a popular file format for audio and video compression developed by the Moving Picture Experts Group.
2 Both disks are 120 mm in diameter and 1.2 mm thick. They also use laser technology to read data.
3 DVDs allow for closer tracks and smaller pits. They can hold more gigabytes of data than CDs.
4 4.7 GB
5 17 GB

3

DVD-ROM	DVD-R
• holds computer data • compatible with old CD-ROMs, video CDs and CD-R disks	• similar in concept to CD-R (recordable), i.e. it can record data only once

DVD Video	DVD + Rewritable
• holds full-length movies • can support eight different languages, 32 subtitles, and various audio formats	• can be erased and reused many times

DIVX
• short for digital video express • format promoted by the film industry • it's like a pay-per-view DVD

4

Addition: also, In addition, Furthermore
Contrast: However, whereas
Result/Effect: thus, so

5

1 while   2 so   3 and   4 Besides
5 on the other hand   6 secondly   7 because of

6

1 A virus entered the computer; as a result many files have been destroyed.
2 Although DVDs and CDs are physically similar in size, their data structure is very different. *or* DVDs and CDs are physically similar in size, although their data structure is very different.

3 Colour, animation and 3D graphics are essential in many applications, for example they're used in art, graphic design and engineering.

4 In computers, RAM memory is temporary; however, the ROM section is permanent.

Unit 13: *Operating systems*

1

1 Everybody	pronoun
2 <u>all</u> programs	determiner
3 each	pronoun
4 <u>each</u> occasion	determiner
5 <u>some</u> books	determiner
6 Nobody	pronoun
7 nothing	pronoun
8 <u>no</u> messages	determiner
9 none	pronoun

2 *Translation*

3 *Translation*
<u>All</u> and <u>both</u> take a plural verb.
<u>None</u> and <u>neither</u> take a singular verb.

4
1 Neither 2 all 3 None 4 both

5
1 Some 2 anything 3 Anybody 4 any 5 some
6 any 7 some 8 somebody 9 something 10 any

6
1 A virus is a piece of software written deliberately to enter your computer and damage your data. Typically it attaches itself to another program and replicates itself trying to 'infect' as many files as possible.
2 The *Jerusalem* virus activates on Friday 13th, displaying a black window on the screen and deleting infected files.
3 *Code Red* was a 'worm'; it replicated itself many times infecting thousands of Web servers.
4 A Trojan horse is a destructive program that disguises itself as a safe program.
5 Viruses can enter a computer in three different ways: (i) via a disk drive, when you insert infected disks or CDs; (ii) via files downloaded from the Web, or (iii) via e-mail attachments.
6 The virus was sent to everyone in your address book.
7 You can protect your system with an anti-virus program such as Norton Anti-virus or McAfee VirusScan.

7
1 b 2 h 3 c 4 a 5 f 6 g 7 e 8 d

Unit 14: *The graphical user interface*

1
1 graphical user interface or GUI
2 computer simulation 3 head-mounted display
4 data glove (or VR glove) 5 flight simulators

2
1 virtual reality 2 virtual interface 3 pictures
4 stereoscopic vision 5 joystick 6 suit
7 exhibitions 8 tiny

3
1 then 2 does 3 do so 4 that 5 ones
6 there 7 one

4 *Possible answer*
A typical graphical user interface today is based on windows, icons and menus. However, scientists are developing a new interface based on virtual reality.

In a virtual interface, you put on a head-mounted display to see the images which give you the feeling of being in a 3-D world.

This interface includes controlling devices such as joysticks, gloves, body suits and motion detectors.

VR systems are used in video games, designs, virtual exhibitions, flight simulation and telepresence systems.

Unit 15: *A walk through word processing*

1
a *Translation*

b	
header:	COMPUTER GAMES
footer:	Page 20
bold text:	**Arcade games** (and other headings)
italic text:	*Sega Dreamcast, Sony PlayStation, Nintendo GameCube, Microsoft XBox*
web link:	www.gamesville.lycos.com
underlined text:	<u>Web servers</u>
word count:	219 words
margin:	left and right margins
inserted picture:	
selected block:	amusement arcade

Times Roman typeface: the text font

2
1 g 2 d 3 c 4 b 5 f 6 a 7 e

3
1 So can I. 2 Nor/Neither do I. 3 So was I.
4 So would I. 5 Neither/Nor did I.

4
1 Oh, I am. 2 Really? I didn't. 3 Oh, I don't.
4 Really? I have. 5 Oh, I will.

5 *Open task*

6 *Open task*

Unit 16: *Spreadsheets*

1

		¹B	U	S	I	N	E	S	S
	²P	A	P	E	R				
			³R	O	W				
			⁴C	E	L	L			
⁵F	O	R	M	U	L	A	S		
			⁶U	P	D	A	T	E	
	⁷W	O	R	K	S	H	E	E	T
	⁸G	R	A	P	H	S			
⁹I	N	V	O	I	C	E	S		
	¹⁰V	A	L	U	E				
		¹¹D	A	T	A	B	A	S	E

2

1 a 2 b 3 c 4 a 5 a

3

1 adverb 2 adjective 3 adjective 4 adverb
5 adjective 6 adverb 7 adverb 8 adjective
9 adverb 10 adjective 11 adjective 12 adverb

4

1 We usually book our holiday through the Web.
2 They are always fighting.
3 He never opens e-mails from strangers.
4 She walks home quickly.
5 I have often been to London.

5

1 Jan works at a computer shop on Saturday mornings.
2 We rarely see rugby on TV these days.
3 She will probably win the race.
4 I ordered a new computer a few weeks ago.

6 Possible answer

We can use e-mail instead of faxes. We usually send and receive a lot of faxed documents from product suppliers and educational authorities, which costs a lot of money. With e-mail, however, we can communicate very efficiently and save money and paper. We can use a spreadsheet program to prepare the school budget and then e-mail it to everyone who needs a copy.

We can use scanning equipment to copy printed information into the computer (e.g. students' and teachers' records, official documentation, etc.); we can then edit it and distribute it electronically.

It's also a good idea to have a school website, where we can post messages and information. There are several advantages: teachers can publish exercises for students to complete online; students can enrol for courses via the website; students can download lessons in electronic format; we can send newsletters to the parents; via a user name and password, parents can download school reports about their children, etc. All these suggestions will help reduce the use of paper.

Unit 17: *Databases*

1 Possible answer

file: program or document created by a user; in a database, it refers to a collection of records.
record: part of a file that holds related data elements (fields)
field: unit of information in a record

2

Fields: 10 fields of text + the photo

3 Possible answer

4

1 d 2 a 3 c 4 e 5 b 6 g 7 f

5

1 Dear Ms Atkinson 2 I am writing
3 I am enclosing 4 We would be grateful if you could
5 Please contact us 6 Yours sincerely

6 Possible answer

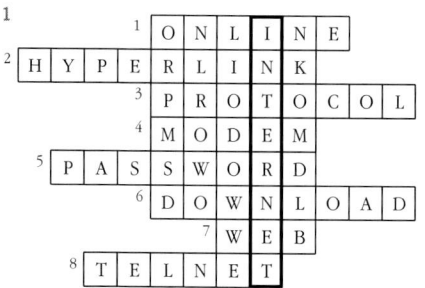

7

1 databases	6 technologies	11 thieves
2 businesses	7 addresses	12 toys
3 facilities	8 taxes	13 physics
4 software	9 media	14 beliefs
5 salaries	10 heroes	15 switches

8

1 Jack's briefcase
2 Russia's influence
3 the influence of the Internet
4 yesterday's news
5 the Houses of Parliament
6 the top of the mountain

9

1 ✓ 2 ✓ 3 ✗ 4 ✓ 5 ✗ 6 ✗ 7 ✓ 8 ✗
3 Kelly's minidisk player
5 the girls' Nintendo GameCube
6 Peter's idea
8 my brother's CDs

Unit 18: *Faces of the Internet*

1

2 *Possible answer*

Robert,

It's Phil's birthday on Saturday and I'd like to arrange a surprise party for him. Can you please help me organize everything?

I'm going to send e-mails inviting friends and classmates to the party. Phil likes reading very much. Shall we buy him a book? I'd also like to get him a nice movie on DVD.

But I can't prepare the food. Could you please make some sandwiches and bring a few drinks? Please don't forget to bring some music CDs.

Give me a ring tomorrow, OK?

Liz

3

1 How old is Peter Morgan?
2 Where does he live?
3 What does he do? / What is his job?
4 What does he use the Internet for? /
  What does he do with the Internet?
5 When did he write a book on e-commerce?
6 What time does he finish work?
7 What does he like doing in his free time?
8 How often does he go to the cinema?

4 *Possible questions*

 1 What is your favourite Internet portal?
 2 What kind of information do you get on the Web?
 3 How many e-mail addresses do you have?
 4 Do you have an anti-virus program?
 5 Do you send instant messages to friends?
 6 Have you ever played games online?
 7 Have you ever bought things over the Net?
 8 Have you ever booked your holiday on the Net?
 9 Is it safe to shop on the Internet?
10 Do you use a mobile phone or PDA to access the Net?
11 Do you ever download electronic music?
12 Do you know how to compress and decompress files?
13 Do you create and design your own Web pages?

Unit 19: *Graphics and design*

1

¹	I	M	A	G	E	S			
²	I	N	T	E	R	F	A	C	E
			³	P	A	L	E	T	T	E
⁴	G	R	A	P	H	S			
				⁵	S	H	A	D	I	N	G
					⁶	P	I	X	E	L
					⁷	I	C	O	N	S
			⁸	D	E	S	I	G	N	E	R

2

1 the process <u>of creating</u> ... Gerund
2 The lady <u>carrying</u> the books ... Present participle
3 <u>Climbing</u> that mountain was <u>exhausting</u>.
  Gerund   Adjective
4 a network <u>linking</u> ... Present participle
5 She was <u>printing</u> ... Present participle
6 full of <u>depressing</u> news ... Adjective
7 <u>Advertising</u> on the web is <u>becoming</u> fashionable.
  Gerund   Present participle

3 *Possible answers*

1 typing the letter / reading the book
2 seeing / watching
3 buying
4 hearing
5 swimming / dancing / listening to MP3 music
6 cooking / washing up / doing it
7 living / travelling / going

4

1 doing 2 visiting 3 protesting 4 laughing
5 Scaling 6 spending 7 performing 8 testing

5 *Possible answer*

I have stopped smoking / drinking alcohol recently.
I must remember to lock the door / to post this letter.
I remember reading comics / playing with my brother when I was a child.
I would like to be an architect / to have a PlayStation.
I can't stand being kept waiting.
I am used to getting up early.
I like jogging / listening to classical music / travelling.

Unit 20: *Desktop publishing*

1

1 desktop 2 layout 3 font 4 import
5 clip art 6 service bureau 7 imagesetters

2

1 a 2 c 3 e 4 d 5 f 6 b

3

a 1 a 2 d 3 i 4 g
b 5 b 6 h 7 e 8 c 9 f
c *Possible answer*

The use of a computer system for all steps of document production, including typing, editing, graphics and printing.

4

1 print<u>er</u>: affixation (suffix); noun
2 <u>re</u>print: affixation (prefix); verb or noun
3 print<u>able</u>: affixation (suffix); adjective
4 print<u>ed</u>: affixation (suffix); verb or adjective
5 print-out: compounding; noun
6 blueprint: compounding; noun
7 <u>im</u>print: affixation (prefix); verb or noun
8 print<u>ing</u>: affixation (suffix); noun or participle
9 footprint: compounding; noun

5

1 electronic mail software
2 a personal computer hardware company
3 a mobile phone industry
4 a page layout application
5 a luxurious modern British car
6 fashionable blue Italian jeans
7 a blue polyester shirt
8 a new French detective film
9 an attractive old French man

Unit 21: *Web design*

1 *Possible answers*
1 Can I use the phone, please?
2 May I read your newspaper, please?
3 Could I park my car in your garage, please?
4 May I send a fax from here, please?
5 May/Could I ask a question?

2 *Possible answers*
1 Can you open the window, please?
2 Would you mind switching on the heater, please?
3 Could you put a music CD on, please?
4 Will you pass me a dictionary, please?
5 Could you speak louder, please?

3 *Possible answers*
1 Would you stop smoking – it's not allowed here.
2 Could you please send me a catalogue of your products?
3 Would you mind translating this web page for me?
4 Can you lend me some money, please?
5 Will you give me the password, please?

4
1 b   2 c   3 a   4 c   5 b

5
1 can   2 was able to   3 could   4 can't   5 must

Unit 22: *Multimedia*

1

	1	F	O	R	M	A	T	S	
2	S	O	U	N	D				
		3	P	L	A	Y	E	R	
	4	O	P	T	I	C	A	L	
5	M	U	S	I	C	A	L		
6	A	N	I	M	A	T	I	O	N
7	H	Y	P	E	R	T	E	X	T
		8	V	I	D	E	O		
		9	E	D	I	T	I	N	G
10	W	E	B	C	A	S	T		

2
1 MP3 is a standard format that compresses audio files for easy transmission over the Net. (It is short for MPEG-1 Audio Layer 3.)
2 Because it offers high compression (files are compressed by a factor of 12), and high-quality sound for little or no cost.
3 An MP3 player.
4 Streaming audio lets you play music directly over the Web (you don't have to wait until the whole file is downloaded).
5 By using a CD ripper (which extracts music tracks from the CD) and an encoder (which turns them into MP3 format).
6 Because a lot of MP3 files are offered free of charge on illegal sites, and record companies may lose a lot of money.

3
1 g   2 h   3 e   4 b   5 c   6 a   7 d   8 f

4
1 b   2 c   3 e   4 a   5 d

5
1 It was <u>so</u> cold <u>that the water froze</u>. = Result
2 Teachers use multimedia software <u>to teach subjects like music and languages</u>. = Purpose
3 Put the CDs <u>wherever you like</u>. = Place
4 <u>If you bring your digital video camera</u>, we can make a movie on my PC. = Condition
5 <u>Even though she has lived in Boston for three years</u>, she can't speak English. = Concession
6 <u>As it was late</u>, we decided to leave. = Reason/cause

6
1 Although Paul Scott is very famous he is unhappy.
2 As her computer doesn't work properly she has decided to format the hard disk.
3 Since he has no money he can't buy a multimedia PC.
4 As soon as she gets paid she'll buy a new PC.
5 Before going to a computer shop he'll look at a brochure.
6 Unless there is a good telephone system, the Internet won't expand.

Unit 23: *Program design*

1

F	C			B	U	G			
L	O			A					E
O	M			S				D	P
W	L	P		I			O		A
C	I			C		C			S
H	L	S			O				C
A	E		P			B			A
R	R						O		L
T								L	
		D	E	B	U	G	G	E	R
P	R	O	G	R	A	M	M	E	R

flowchart   compiler   BASIC   Pascal   bug
debugger   programmer   LISP   COBOL   code

2
1 program   2 flowchart   3 language   4 compiled
5 errors   6 debugging   7 documentation

3
1 A flowchart is a diagram that uses standardized symbols showing the logical relationship between the various parts of the program.
2 They write source code in a high-level computer language.
3 'Debugging' is detecting and correcting errors (bugs) in a program.

4

1 to meet   2 spending   3 to do   4 understand

5 (to) remove   6 living   7 to buy

5

1 b   2 c   3 b   4 c   5 a   6 b   7 a   8 a

6

2 The manager reminded Freya to turn off the computer.

3 Ludwig invited Pedro to have a coffee.

4 The pilot asked the passengers to fasten their seat belts.

5 The teacher ordered the students to stop fighting.

6 Eva advised Marta not to smoke so much.

7 The bank robbers told the cashier not to make a sound.

8 The engineer warned the employees not to touch the cables because it was dangerous.

Unit 24: *Languages*

1

See examples of the passive in exercise 2.

The passive is formed by the verb *be* in the appropriate tense and the past participle of the main verb.

2

Past simple: was arrested, was accused, was fined, was charged, was released

Present perfect: has been sent

Past perfect: had been caught

***Will* future:** will be introduced

NOTE:

Present simple: It is reported

3

1 were built   2 were printed   3 was written

4 was invented   5 were discovered

6 was broadcast   7 was used   8 was painted

4

1 are made   2 is cut   3 are treated   4 are built

5 is tested   6 is inserted

5

1 is often used   2 was developed

3 are made / were made   4 are being replaced

5 must be developed   6 has just been found

7 will be introduced

6 Possible answer

First, the car is designed on computer with a CAD program. Next, in the stamping plant, the metal sheets are pressed and cut into the shapes of the car frame. Then the metal parts are joined by welding robots.

The other parts (engine, wheels, brakes, etc.) are assembled on the frame on the assembly line. After that, the frame is sent to the paint shop.

Next, the tyres are inflated and the seats are placed in the car. Then, IT devices are included.

Now, the vehicle is ready to be checked and tested at the track. Finally, the cars are distributed and sold.

Unit 25: *The Java revolution*

1

1 e   2 f   3 a   4 d   5 c   6 b

2

1 the abacus

2 Augusta Ada

3 Second generation computers used transistors instead of vacuum tubes.

4 Intel

5 MS-DOS

6 the Apple Macintosh

7 1991

8 Sun Microsystems

3 Translation

4

Regular past tenses in *-ed*: emerged, allowed, invented, started, used, designed, released, founded, produced, launched, created.

Irregular past tenses: was, read, built, were, became, sold, wrote

5

Last Monday she didn't phone her parents.

Last Tuesday she wrote an e-mail to a webpal; she didn't watch TV.

Last Wednesday she didn't repair the optical drive; she visited her friend in hospital.

Last Thursday she didn't read the *Financial Times*; she sent a postcard to a friend.

Last Friday she had lunch with her boss; she didn't go to her German class.

Last Saturday she bought a DVD-R drive for her brother.

Last Sunday she downloaded some music from the Net.

6

Past progressive

7

a **Past simple:** broke, did … do, told, was.

Past progressive: were … doing, was sitting.

b

1 A: I realized I had a computer virus on my PC.

 B: Really? What were you doing?

 A: I was typing an invoice for a client.

 B: And what did you do about it?

 A: Fortunately, I had an anti-virus program; so I checked the system and destroyed the virus!

2 A: Someone stole my wallet.

 B: Oh! What were you doing?

 A: I was walking through the gates into the football stadium.

 B: And what did you do about it?

 A: I reported it to the police.

3 A: My grandfather saw a UFO.

 B: Really? What was he doing?

 A: Well, he was driving his car on an abandoned road at night.

 B: And what did he do about it?

 A: He was very frightened, so he drove straight home.

Unit 26: *Jobs in computing*

1 *Possible answer*

Webmaster
- Experience using HTML and Java
- Knowledge of FrontPage (web editor) or equivalent
- Knowledge of Adobe PDF and Photoshop (an advantage)

Computer sales assistant
- Knowledge of operating systems and peripherals
- Some experience in customer relations may be useful
- A driving licence is essential

2

a Webmaster

b

1 completed   2 did   3 learnt   4 studied
5 spent   6 have worked / have been working
7 have been   8 have used / have been using

3

1 have just sent   2 Have you ever worked
3 saw   4 finished   5 Have you received
6 got married   7 has been

4

1 yet   2 yet   3 already   4 for   5 ago   6 since

5

1 has been complaining   2 have been working
3 has just passed   4 have you written
5 have interviewed   6 has been writing
7 Have you been waiting

6 *Possible answer*

Dear Sir/Madam,

I am writing to apply for the post of 'Computer sales assistant' which was advertised in the Evening News on April 3rd.

At school, I did three A-levels in English, Maths and Physics. After I left school in 1998, I did an IT course at Cardiff Polytechnic.

I have in-depth knowledge of the most popular operating systems, including MS Windows, Mac OS and Linux. I am proficient in Windows applications, particularly Microsoft Office, so I am familiar with word processing, spreadsheet and database programs.

For the last two years I have worked as a data entry operator. I have also been responsible for installing and testing PCs and all sorts of hardware devices.

In my free time, I love surfing the Web and listening to music. I have a driving licence and car and I enjoy travelling. I get on well with people.

I enclose a curriculum vitae. I will be available for an interview at any time.

I look forward to hearing from you.

Yours faithfully,
Angela Russell

Unit 27: *Electronic communications*

1

Modem:	MOdulator-DEModulator
kbps:	kilobits per second
ISP:	Internet Service Provider
ADSL:	Asymmetric Digital Subscriber Line
BBS:	Bulletin Board System
FTP:	File Transfer Protocol
IRC:	Internet Relay Chat

2

1 To log on to the Net, he just types his username and password.
2 e-mail, Web search, new software, printing services, DVD, games, etc.
3 It's faster than a conventional modem; you can make phone calls at the same time.
4 Because she is writing a project on IT applications and she wants to look up some terms.
5 He recommends www.webopedia.com

3

1 b   2 d   3 f   4 e   5 a   6 c

4

1 b   2 h   3 a   4 d   5 g   6 e   7 c   8 f

5

1 carries out   2 run out   3 sort out   4 back up
5 takes up   6 give away   7 plug into   8 make up

6

1 d   2 a   3 b   4 c   5 f   6 e

Unit 28: *Internet issues*

1

2

	1	U	S	E	R	N	A	M	E	
2	I	N	T	R	A	N	E	T		
3	S	E	C	U	R	I	T	Y		
		4	C	O	O	K	I	E	S	
				5	S	Q	L			
		6	V	I	R	U	S	E	S	
		7	F	I	R	E	W	A	L	L
		8	F	I	L	T	E	R		
9	E	N	C	R	Y	P	T	I	O	N
		10	H	A	C	K	E	R		

1969	The US Defence Advanced Research Projects Agency establishes ARPANET, the precursor to the Internet.
1971	Ray Tomlinson invents an e-mail program.
1983	The most important networks (ARPANET, MILnet and CSnet) are interconnected.
1988	Jarkko Oikarinen develops the system known as Internet Relay Chat (IRC).
1991	CERN develops the World Wide Web.
1993	Marc Andreesen develops *Mosaic*, the first program that allows users to surf the Web.
1999	Online banking, e-commerce and MP3 music become fashionable.
2001	Napster lets users download MP3 music files. But a federal judge rules that Napster's technology is an infringement on the copyright of music.

3

The US ARPA established

Ray Tomlinson invented ... the @ sign was chosen ...

ARPANET made

V. Cerf and B. Kahn published

... forum (newsgroups) constituted ...

BITNET provided

TCP-IP was adopted

The most important ... were interconnected

The DNS was created

Jarkko Oikarinen developed

CERN developed

Philip Zimmerman wrote ... protected

Marc Andreesen developed, ... allowed

Commercial online systems started

RealNetworks created, ... let

Netscape ... started

Java ... were

The Internet 2 network was born

Online banking, ... became

Napster let ... ruled ... was

4

1 d   2 b   3 a   4 c

5

1 had been waiting   2 had you been working

3 had been designing   4 had been hacking

5 had been using   6 had been smoking

6 *Possible answers*

They had disconnected the security alarm and video camera.

They had broken the window.

They had switched on the computers.

They had stolen bank account details and confidential data.

They had taken the money.

They had stolen bank notes and coins.

Unit 29: *LANs and WANs*

1

1 a   2 c   3 b   4 c   5 a   6 c   7 a

2

1 by   2 at   3 inside   4 between

5 on   6 in   7 out of   8 into

3 *Possible answers*

In this office, the computers are connected in a small network.

They're linked to a printer, a fax and the telephone line.

On the left there is a fax machine on the table. The printer is next to the fax. There is a wastepaper basket beside the table.

In the centre there are two desks and two employees.

The man is typing at the computer. There are some CDs and a cup of coffee on his desk. The tower PC is under the desk. There is a shelf next to the door and a picture above the shelf. He has a noticeboard on the wall to his right.

The woman is talking on the phone. She has a calculator on her desk. There is a poster on the wall next to the window. There is a flower pot between the two desks.

There is a carpet in the middle of the room and an armchair in front of it. There is a computer magazine on the carpet. There is a bookcase on the right, under the window, and a filing cabinet on the right of the bookcase.

4

1 What is she talking about?

2 Who is he going out with?

3 Who did you send the fax to?

4 Who does your brother work for?

5

1 The city centre is difficult to get to.

2 He is nice to talk to.

3 Small cars are uncomfortable to travel in.

4 Dina is boring to play chess with.

Unit 30: *New technologies*

1

1 a   2 b   3 c   4 a   5 b

2 *Possible answers*

1 He is going to write a letter.

2 He is going to check for viruses.

3 She is going to take a picture of them.

4 They are going to get into the car.

5 He is going to score a goal.

3

1 are going

2 will love

3 are you travelling

4 are flying

5 are staying

6 are visiting

7 will probably stop / are probably stopping

8 will just relax

4 *Possible answers*

1 In 20 years' time some people will travel to Mars; there will be hotels in outer space.

2 We'll watch interactive TV and navigate the Internet at the same time.

3 Mobile phones will be used to control activities inside the house (e.g. to turn off the heating system, switch on the washing machine, etc.).

4 Geneticists will use smart computers to make humans more intelligent.

5 Energy control systems will regulate the use of electricity in homes.

5 *Translation*

List of irregular verbs

You should revise the most important **IRREGULAR VERBS**.

A — All three forms alike

Base	Past simple	Past participle	Translation
bet	bet	bet	
cost	cost	cost	....
cut	cut	cut	....
hit	hit	hit	....
hurt	hurt	hurt	....
set	set	set	....
let	let	let	....
put	put	put	....
shut	shut	shut	....
spread	spread	spread	....
read	read /red/	read /red/	....

B — Base = Past simple

Base	Past simple	Past participle	Translation
beat	beat	beaten	....

C — Past simple = Past participle

Base	Past simple	Past participle	Translation
bend	bent	bent	
bleed	bled	bled	....
bring	brought	brought	....
build	built	built	....
buy	bought	bought	....
catch	caught	caught	....
deal	dealt	dealt	....
feed	fed	fed	....
feel	felt	felt	....
fight	fought	fought	....
find	found	found	....
get	got	got	....
hang	hung	hung	....
have	had	had	....
hear	heard	heard	....
hold	held	held	....
keep	kept	kept	....
lay	laid	laid	....
lead	led	led	....
learn	learnt	learnt	....
leave	left	left	....
lend	lent	lent	....
light	lit	lit	....
lose	lost	lost	....
make	made	made	....
mean	meant	meant	....
meet	met	met	....
pay	paid	paid	....
say	said	said	....
sell	sold	sold	....
send	sent	sent	....
shine	shone	shone	....
shoot	shot	shot	....
sit	sat	sat	....
sleep	slept	slept	....
spend	spent	spent	....
stand	stood	stood	....
stick	stuck	stuck	....
strike	struck	struck	....
sweep	swept	swept	....
teach	taught	taught	....
tell	told	told	....
think	thought	thought	....
understand	understood	understood	....
win	won	won	....

D Base = Past participle

Base	Past simple	Past participle	Translation
become	became	become	....
come	came	come	....
run	ran	run	....

E All three forms different

Base	Past simple	Past participle	Translation
arise	arose	arisen	....
awake	awoke	awoken	....
be	was/were	been	....
begin	began	begun	....
bite	bit	bitten	....
blow	blew	blown	....
break	broke	broken	....
choose	chose	chosen	....
do	did	done	....
draw	drew	drawn	....
drink	drank	drunk	....
drive	drove	driven	....
eat	ate	eaten	....
fall	fell	fallen	....
fly	flew	flown	....
forbid	forbade	forbidden	....
forget	forgot	forgotten	....
forgive	forgave	forgiven	....
freeze	froze	frozen	....
give	gave	given	....
go	went	gone	....
grow	grew	grown	....
hide	hid	hidden	....
know	knew	known	....
lie	lay	lain	....
ride	rode	ridden	....
ring	rang	rung	....
rise	rose	risen	....
see	saw	seen	....
shake	shook	shaken	....
show	showed	shown	....
shrink	shrank	shrunk	....
sing	sang	sung	....
sink	sank	sunk	....
speak	spoke	spoken	....
steal	stole	stolen	....
swear	swore	sworn	....
swim	swam	swum	....
take	took	taken	....
tear	tore	torn	....
throw	threw	thrown	....
wake	wokc	woken	....
wear	wore	worn	....
withdraw	withdrew	withdrawn	....
write	wrote	written	....

Acknowledgements

From the author:
I would like to express my gratitude to teachers and students of
I.E.S. Pilar Lorengar, Zaragoza.
My special thanks to Angel Benedí for his advice on technical aspects;
Will Capel for his help and support;
Alison Silver for editing the typescript.

The author and publishers would like to thank the following for
permission to reproduce photographs and other illustrative material.

Key: *(t)* = top; *(c)* = centre; *(b)* = bottom; *(l)* = left; *(r)* = right.

Cartoons: pp.7, 9, 13, 19, 25, 33, 37, 39, 40, 43 www.cartoonstock.com
Photographs: p.10 The MovieStore Collection; pp.12 *bl*, 55 Photodisk
Green; p.12 *bc* Microsoft; p.12 *br* Swann Communications Ltd
www.swann.com.au; p.16 *l, cl* Epson; p.16 *cr* Brand X; p.16 *r*
A. Green/Griffin Technology Inc.; p.20 Courtesy of Apple;
p.22 Hewlett-Packard Company; p.33 Corbis/R. Ressmeyer;
p.41 Taxi/L. Bray; p.47 Departmento de Artes Gráficas, I.E.S.
Pilar Lorengar; other photos provided by Santiago Remacha Esteras.

Illustrations by Martin Fish

Picture research by Mark Ruffle

Designed and produced by Kamae Design, Oxford